AMERICAN HIGHER EDUCATION

American Higher Education

An International Perspective

V. R. CARDOZIER
Professor of Higher Education,
University of Texas at Austin

Avebury

Aldershot · Brookfield USA · Hong Kong · Singapore · Sydney

Published by

Avebury
Gower Publishing Company Limited
Gower House, Croft Road
Aldershot, Hants GU11 3HR
England

Gower Publishing Company
Old Post Road
Brookfield, Vermont 05036
USA

ISBN 0 566 05428 0

Printed and bound in Great Britain by
Athanaeum Press Limited, Newcastle upon Tyne

Contents

Figures and map

Tables

Tables

Preface

When I first travelled to Europe many years ago and visited universities and other institutions of higher education I was struck by the differences between European and American higher education. It was not only differences in structures, organization, administration, finance, governance and teaching but differences in national attitudes towards higher education and its role in the life of the country.

As a student of higher education I knew something of the higher education system of each country I visited but, in each case, I would have benefited greatly by a single volume that explained the higher education system of the country comprehensively. Then and in subsequent visits, as I talked with Europeans, both educators and others, I found them perplexed and curious about American colleges and universities.

This book is an attempt to explain American higher education to those whose understanding of it is limited. Unless they are higher education scholars, Americans and others who are already acquainted with colleges and universities in the United States should find this book illuminating, especially with respect to aspects about which they are unclear. Those whose experience has been limited to a single type of institution, for example, private liberal arts colleges or comprehensive state universities, will find the comprehensive treatment of all types of higher education institutions instructive.

However this book is written primarily for non-American readers. Whether the reader is visiting America or planning such a visit, or is simply interested in gaining a thorough picture of American higher education, he or she should find the book enlightening.

I have tried to keep in mind the orientations of readers in other countries and their perceptions of higher education and to deal with each aspect in a manner to which they can relate. Even so readers outside the United States will need to make a few translations as they read. In several cases I have used in the American sense terms which have different meanings in some other countries; for example, college or school, not faculty, refers to an organizational unit in a university; faculty refers to teachers as a group or category; tuition refers to fees paid for instruction; gymnasium is a building for sports activities; professor is the highest academic rank but the term professors is sometimes used to refer to teachers generically.

Europeans and others outside the United States are often baffled by the number and frequency of tests and examinations American students must take as they progress through their periods of study. The accumulation of credits to qualify for the first degree without a final comprehensive examination is also puzzling.

A visitor to the United States will also wonder about a system in which government exercises so little control over colleges and universities, that each of the fifty states sets its own rules and regulations for public colleges and universities, without direction from the federal government; and that private institutions, which constitute more than half the total, are largely free of direction from either state or federal government.

They wonder too about a system that insists its primary mission is teaching but in which teachers rarely fail to gain tenure because of poor teaching yet frequently fail to do so because of inadequate research and publication.

Readers in countries in which all or almost all institutions of higher education are governed by a national ministry of education should find novel the American approach to governing institutions with boards of trustees composed of laymen whose responsibilities and authority sometimes seem ambiguous.

British university and polytechnic teachers are aghast at the large student-teacher ratios in American colleges and universities, usually seventeen or eighteen students per teacher in a research university and as high as thirty in a comprehensive state college or university.

The American community college is a unique institution that can be called higher education only in part, as viewed from the European perspective. Originally founded in the latter part of the last century to provide the first two years of university study, it began to take on additional responsibilities after the Second World War. By 1980 half its students were enrolled in vocational and technical programmes not usually classified as higher education. Community colleges provide a wide range of informal continuing education classes — academic, occupational and recreational — plus a considerable number of community service activities.

American colleges and universities are reflections of American culture, ideals and political attitudes, the belief that everyone should have a chance to achieve to the limit of his or her talents. As a consequence community colleges and some degree-granting colleges and universities practise open admissions, requiring few qualifications for admission. At the same time the American system includes some of the most intellectually demanding institutions in the world.

I have attempted to picture the entire higher education system in the United States including limitations and deficiencies. If any has been omitted it was not intentional for it is my aim to present a balanced view of the total enterprise.

Broad topics such as structure, organization, governance and finance are examined but I recognize that these alone would not present a complete picture of American higher education. Therefore I have included procedures, practices and details of day-to-day activities of institutions, which when combined help one to gain a more comprehensive understanding of American colleges and universities.

Much of the writing about American higher education focuses largely on a small number of institutions, usually the highly prestigious private universities and liberal arts colleges and the leading public research universities. It is true that these institutions serve as models and set standards for higher education generally; however they represent only a minority of institutions in the United States. I have attempted in this book more nearly to balance treatment of different types of colleges and universities.

There are almost 3300 institutions of post-secondary education in the United States and since no national ministry governs them, not only private but public institutions too have considerable autonomy and freedom to develop as they see fit: hence there are vast differences among institutions and types of institution. As we consider generalizations about American higher education in this book, it should be remembered that such statements are applicable generally but not necessarily to every institution.

Reference to higher education in America as a system might be debatable when compared to countries in which all higher education is under the direction of a central ministry. Yet despite its diversified structure of authority and control and sources of financial support, American higher education can be considered a system in the sense that its various components share many things in common and are linked in many ways.

I owe a debt of gratitude to untold numbers of people who have contributed indirectly to this undertaking, and to my wife, Nancy Fyfe Cardozier, whose contributions as critic were invaluable.

Austin, Texas   V.R. Cardozier
October 1986

State Outline of the United States

1 History and development

American higher education began in 1636 with the founding of Harvard College across the Charles river from Boston in Massachusetts. Harvard was not only the first American college but became the model for others to follow and is today the pre-eminent university in America.

It was almost sixty years before the founding of the next college — William and Mary College in Virginia. Still, there was no rush to establish colleges. In 1701 Yale College was founded, then the University of Pennsylvania in 1740, Princeton University in 1746, Columbia and Brown universities in 1754, Rutgers in 1764 and Dartmouth in 1769, all founded under other names. At the outbreak of the American Revolution (1775) these nine were the only colleges in America.

The main purpose of creating colleges was to train clergymen. Among the early colonists were a sizeable number of educated men — more than 125 Oxford and Cambridge graduates — who were influential in the founding of the colleges. In addition to training clergymen the colleges also declared their purpose to include the training of civic and business leaders; but they were decidedly oriented towards the clergy. The American colonists were a pious people. Deep religious commitment and public demonstration of it were present everywhere.

With a strong representation of Oxford and Cambridge men among their founders the early colleges had a distinctly English flavour. Harvard was modelled on Emmanuel College, Cambridge. William and Mary, founded by a Virginia immigrant who had studied at Edinburgh and Aberdeen, initially adopted the Scottish model but in time took on characteristics of the English college.

After the American Revolution the United States began to find its identity as a nation and colleges were created more rapidly. Several were founded before 1800 including the first state college, which later became the University of Georgia (1785), plus the University of North Carolina (1795) and state institutions in Tennessee and Vermont.

The curriculum in the early colleges was classical. At Harvard it included Latin, Greek, Hebrew, rhetoric, religion, logic, mathematics, natural philosophy (physics) and moral philosophy. Colleges founded during the remainder of that century departed little from the Harvard curriculum. Religion and church attendance were stressed. Attendance at morning and evening prayers and Sunday church services was mandatory.

The first half of the nineteenth century saw a rush to establish colleges. A few were established by state governments but the large majority were the work of churches and religious groups. Between 1800 and 1860 hundreds of so-called colleges were opened; many of them were not colleges in today's terms but in fact secondary schools, and in some cases schools that offered study equivalent to one or two years of college-level education. Since no governmental approval was required religious bodies set up colleges in small towns and rural areas throughout the country, but most of them disappeared within a short time owing to lack of students, lack of money, poor location and a variety of other reasons. At the beginning of the Civil War (1861) there were about 250 colleges in the US, most of them far too small, poorly financed and lacking academic quality; yet about 185 still exist today.

Because most of them were founded by religious bodies — mostly Protestant since the Catholic college movement was to come later — the colleges continued to be religious in character. However compulsory church attendance began to disappear early in the second half of the nineteenth century. Harvard eliminated compulsory chapel attendance in 1871, Columbia in 1891, and Johns Hopkins, Chicago and Stanford universities made chapel attendance voluntary when they opened. Except for colleges with close church affiliation, compulsory religious activities had been eliminated in most institutions by early in the twentieth century.

Throughout most of the seventeenth and eighteenth centuries not only were all college presidents clergymen but so were most of the faculty (teachers). Most of the graduates in the first hundred years after the founding of Harvard became clergymen.

Two hundred years after the founding of the first college the curriculum was still classical in most institutions but there were exceptions.

Union College, founded in Schenectady, New York in 1795, permitted electives in curricula and by 1839 it had the second largest enrolment in the country.

Change came slowly. When colleges began to discontinue requiring Greek for admission, loud protestations were heard from faculty who feared standards were being destroyed. Yale, when offered a professorship in French in 1778, rejected it for fear it would corrupt the curriculum, yet the following year Columbia began to offer French. Other colleges substituted French for Hebrew (Harvard, 1787), persuaded in part by the role France had played in the American Revolution.

Early in the nineteenth century laymen were criticizing colleges for adhering to the classical curriculum because it was so far removed from life and from what students would do after college. In 1827 the Connecticut legislature sharply criticized Yale for its curriculum but the Yale faculty issued a staunch defence of classical studies, arguing that they developed a disciplined mind and built character. At Harvard Latin remained the language of conversation until 1731 and commencement was held in Latin until 1760.

By the 1830s curriculum changes were under way. Colleges were reluctant to abandon the classical curriculum but some offered in addition a literary curriculum that included more modern studies. About this time several technical institutes were founded and before the beginning of the Civil War several states had established agricultural colleges. Clearly the public was beginning to expect colleges to teach something of practical use.

Land-grant colleges

Nothing influenced the development and expansion of higher education for the masses more than the land-grant college movement. In 1862 the US Congress passed the Morrill Act which directed that each state be given federally owned land (30 000 acres for each member of Congress for that state) for the purpose of a public college to teach agriculture and the mechanical arts (engineering). While the land when sold by each state produced only modest sums they were sufficient to stimulate state legislatures to establish what became known as A & M colleges.

Several states that had already established state colleges converted them to land-grant colleges, others founded new institutions and six states in the north-eastern part of the country, which had long relied on private colleges and were less favourably disposed towards tax supported colleges, contracted with private colleges to offer land-grant college programmes. All these have since transferred the land-grant programmes to state colleges — since established — except the state of New York whose land-grant colleges of agriculture and home economics are located at Cornell University and college of forestry at Syracuse University, both private institutions.

From the beginning the land-grant colleges stressed practical training. Farmers' sons began to attend college and the notion spread that college was available to ordinary people. In a few short years there was a transformation in American colleges concerning who could attend, the purpose of college, the curriculum and role of research.

Soon after the beginning of the land-grant college movement the university movement, which stressed research, got under way. The people involved in developing land-grant colleges soon realized that without research there was little for them to teach, other than practical experience and folklore, so in 1887 the Congress passed a law authorizing funds for each land-grant college to establish a research unit which came to be called an agricultural experiment station. The agricultural experiment stations produced research findings that revolutionized American agriculture and are still important components of land-grant institutions. They are partly financed by the US government through the US Department of Agriculture and partly by the legislature in each state.

In 1890 the Congress passed another law providing a small amount of continuing funding for teaching in land-grant colleges and specified that Negroes, who had been freed from slavery in 1865, could not be excluded. At that time separate schools and colleges were maintained for Negroes in the southern part of the US so each of the southern states where slavery had existed before 1865 established separate land-grant colleges. Although blacks have been free to enrol in formerly all-white schools and colleges for many years the formerly all-black land-grant colleges — which now enrol a minority of white students — still thrive because a large percentage of black students prefer to attend them.

The last major step in land-grant college development came in 1914. Agriculture leaders realized that if farmers were to benefit from the research findings of state agricultural experiment stations, there must be some organized way of getting the information to them. The Congress created the Agricultural Extension Service as an agency of the land-grant college in each state. The Agricultural Extension Service stationed men and women trained in agriculture and home economics in each county[1] of every state to bring results of agricultural and homemaking research to farmers and farm families. Later, agents were added to train farm youth in agriculture and homemaking, citizenship and leadership through an organization known as the 4-H Club. As

America has become more urbanized the county agricultural extension staffs have extended their services to urban and rural non-farm people. The federal government pays about one-third and the states about two-thirds of the cost of operating the Agricultural Extension Service in each state.

In twenty-nine states the land-grant college, that is, the formerly all-white land-grant institution, is combined with the premier or flagship university, but in twenty states the land-grant institution is separate. Before the Second World War the twenty separate land-grant institutions offered degree programmes in the sciences and other fields that supported programmes in agriculture and engineering but little in the liberal arts and other professional fields. After the war they began to expand curricula, partly owing to the bulge of veterans enrolling, and soon they were offering most of the curricula found in universities. Pennsylvania State College and Michigan State College replaced the college in their names with university in the 1950s and gradually all the other land-grant colleges changed their titles to university.

The university movement

With a few exceptions teachers in colonial colleges were trained to bachelor's degree only. Some of the graduates remained at the college, usually while waiting for a vacant pulpit, and continued their studies while serving as teaching assistants; in due course some of them were awarded master's degrees. More often the master's degree was awarded to graduates who maintained a good character for three years after graduation and paid a fee.

When Thomas Jefferson established the University of Virginia in 1824 he recruited a number of European trained scholars, particularly graduates of German universities who held the PhD degree. Other institutions appointed European scholars, especially in the sciences, and gradually the idea spread that college faculty could benefit from graduate study in Europe.

Throughout the nineteenth century a growing number of Americans went to Germany to pursue advanced study. Several German universities were popular with Americans but the University of Berlin attracted the largest number. It has been estimated that by the end of the century more than 10 000 Americans had taken advanced study in German universities.

These scholars brought back to America a profound belief in research and scholarship and were to have a major impact on American higher education. In the last quarter of the nineteenth century a considerable number of universities were established and old colleges changed to universities, both in name and in their programmes. Scientific truth began to replace revealed truth; and PhD trained scientists to replace the older faculty, who were unacquainted with this new approach to knowledge.

In 1876 Johns Hopkins University was founded in Baltimore with the avowed purpose of being a research and graduate education institution although it offered a small undergraduate programme from the beginning. Its faculty, mostly trained to PhD level, attracted some of the most brilliant students in America and very quickly the university had an effect on American higher education.

Few universities had more impact however than the University of Chicago, which was founded in 1892 and also stressed research, scholarship and graduate education. William Rainey Harper, the founding president, had received the PhD degree from a German university. An ebullient personality and tireless worker, he succeeded quickly in making the university one of the premier research universities in the country.

By the middle of the nineteenth century the trend towards research and advanced study caused many American colleges to consider changes. The first earned master's degree, based on a programme of study rather than a period of time, was awarded by the University of Michigan in 1853 and the first earned PhD degree was awarded by Yale University in 1861. Johns Hopkins University and the University of Chicago became major centres of PhD study. By the latter part of the century so had Harvard and it soon became the leading graduate university in the country.

The last quarter of the nineteenth century also saw the establishment of state universities in additional states and colleges that would later become universities. The university movement influenced these institutions considerably; most of them not only adopted the university name but in time became universities in fact.

Normal schools and teacher's colleges

At the end of the nineteenth century the demand for teachers for elementary (primary) and secondary schools expanded the demand for teacher training, leading to the development of two-year normal schools. The European distinction between university training for secondary school teachers and teacher's college for primary school teachers has never existed in the United States. Both elementary and secondary school teachers were trained in two-year normal schools.

Early in the twentieth century some of the two-year normal schools began to be converted to four-year colleges, and a few became junior colleges. The four-year institutions were called teacher's colleges but soon began to offer curricula in other fields of study. The baby boom following the Second World War placed pressure on the teacher's colleges to turn out increased numbers of teachers, which they did along with universities and private colleges which also prepare teachers.

In the 1960s when the post-war baby boom began to arrive on college campuses, state legislatures were under pressure to establish new institutions to serve these students. The obvious solution was to convert the teacher's colleges into institutions with broadly based curricula, which the legislatures did. All the teacher's colleges became state colleges or state universities and for the most part each serves primarily the region of the state in which it is located.

The role of the Church

Although the first state college was established in 1785 it was not until the latter part of the nineteenth century that public higher education became significant in America. All the early colleges were established by religious bodies or by laymen who were interested in the training of clergy.

While there were a few private non-denominational colleges and institutes established in the first half of the nineteenth century, the large majority were sponsored by religious denominations. For the first 200 years the Presbyterians and Congregationalists were most active in establishing colleges, then the Methodists and Baptists stepped up their college founding. Other denominations, particularly Lutherans, Episcopalians, Quakers and Universalists, got involved. The Catholics were late-comers in founding colleges, but as Catholic immigrants began to arrive from Ireland and continental Europe the Catholic Church joined in, eventually establishing more than 300 colleges, universities, seminaries and schools of theology. Before the Civil War there were only a dozen or so Catholic colleges; after 1865 Catholic colleges and universities were founded in large numbers.

Teaching and administration of the early Catholic colleges were almost entirely in the hands of the clergy. While clergy dominated the early Protestant colleges, by the latter part of the nineteenth century laymen constituted a majority. However the tradition of a clergyman serving as president persisted until the end of the nineteenth century in many Protestant colleges and universities and indeed the presidency of many church-related institutions is held by a clergyman today. It was not until 1899 that Yale University had a non-clergyman as president and Princeton's first non-clergy president was in 1902.

The early colleges commonly received subsidies from governmental agencies but these were usually special grants. Regular annual appropriations were rare although the dedication of income from a specific tax or fee was not uncommon. For example, in the early years of Harvard College, the General Court of Massachusetts dedicated income from a ferry to Harvard and later toll charges when a bridge replaced the ferry. Public subsidies to private colleges began to disappear as the nineteenth century matured. After 1865 the founding of public colleges grew rapidly and states directed tax funds to the new state-supported institutions.

Community/junior colleges

At the end of the nineteenth century a few private colleges offering only two years of college-level study had been established; they were mostly 'finishing schools' for young women. When the University of Chicago was established in 1892 its president created a lower division and an upper division of undergraduate study, the first two years to consist of general education and the last two of specialized study. Later he met school superintendents from the area surrounding Chicago and urged them to establish junior colleges in connection with the public schools so that students who came to the University of Chicago could enter as juniors.

This led to the establishment of the first public junior college in America at Joliet, Illinois in 1901. Four years later the California legislature passed legislation authorizing public school districts in that state to establish junior colleges as part of the public schools.

Early junior colleges offered only courses that paralleled the first two years of senior colleges and universities and, for the most part, enrolled only students who were preparing to transfer and pursue a bachelor's degree, although many students did not actually transfer. This pattern continued until well after the Second World War. When the expansion in enrolment came in the 1960s junior colleges expanded too and many new ones opened to accommodate millions of additional students.

At the same time there was a growing demand for vocational and technical training of a kind previously associated with trade schools. In the 1920s and 1930s most states had created trade schools where students could prepare for a large number of different jobs that required skill training — auto mechanics, carpentry, sheet metal work, welding, plus secretarial and clerical training, and so on.

By the 1960s this list had been expanded by dozens of technical skills involving computers, electronics, medical and dental technology and many more. Some of these were offered in trade schools but in some states the junior colleges were asked to assume responsibility for providing training in dozens of vocational and technical skills. The 1970s saw vocational and technical training expand very rapidly. The number of junior colleges grew from 527 in 1950 to 1274 in 1980, and enrolment in vocational and technical education equalled the numbers enrolled in academic and general education programmes.

Role of philanthropy

Except for federal land-grants, government support of higher education was modest until well into the nineteenth century. Philanthropy was the major source of funds for the establishment of virtually all the early colleges, although most of the gifts were small.

Harvard College was established in 1636 without notable gifts. The first came from John Harvard, a graduate of Emmanuel College, Cambridge, upon his death in 1638; the trustees of the college renamed it for him the following year. Harvard depended largely on small gifts for many years, and no single individual made substantial gifts in its early years. John Harvard's gift provided only £395. One of the larger early gifts came from John Hollis, a wealthy London merchant who left £75 000 to Harvard in 1731 (Curti and Nash, 1965).

The predecessor of Yale University began with a gift of only £562 from Elihu Yale, a Londoner who had become wealthy in India. William and Mary College in Virginia, the second college established in America (1693), benefited greatly from gifts but its beginning was made possible when a Virginian who had gone to England to secure a charter for the college was able to persuade the Crown to award it a 20 000 acre endowment, £2000 of Virginia quit rents, a tax of a penny a pound on tobacco sold from Virginia and Maryland and proceeds from the office of the surveyor-general.

In the first half of the nineteenth century a large number of colleges were established and partially financed by religious denominations but most collapsed due to lack of funds and students. Large donations to establish colleges and universities or to expand and support them began in the last half of the nineteenth century. John D. Rockefeller, the founder of Standard Oil Company, provided funds for the establishment of the University of Chicago (1892) and continued to provide additional funds for several years. Cornelius Vanderbilt donated $500 000 to tiny Central University in Nashville, Tennessee, when it was established in 1872; in 1873 the trustees changed the name of the institution to Vanderbilt University. Vanderbilt later donated another $500 000 and his heirs gave $10 million additionally.

When he died in 1874 Johns Hopkins of Baltimore, Maryland left

$3.5 million worth of railway shares and property of approximately equal value which trustees used to establish Johns Hopkins University (1876).

Stanford University in California opened in 1891 with gifts from Leland Stanford, the railway magnate, and although the university struggled for several years its fortunes rose later with the rapid escalation in value of gifts of land from Stanford and his wife.

Paul Tulane, a New Orleans businessman, gave more than $1 million, including considerable property, to a group of trustees who created the university that bears his name in that city, absorbing in the process the small struggling University of Louisiana.

The second half of the nineteenth century saw the establishment of many colleges for women, all with donations and bequests — Vassar, Wellesley, Bryn Mawr, Smith and women's colleges that were affiliated with established universities, for example, Pembroke (Brown University), Radcliffe (Harvard), Barnard (Columbia), and Sophie Newcomb (Tulane).

The same period also saw the establishment of a large number of colleges for blacks. In addition to Howard University, established by the federal government, and several state supported colleges in the South, several colleges for blacks were established with gifts from individuals or philanthropic foundations, including Fisk University and Meharry Medical College in Nashville, Tennessee; Tuskegee Institute in Alabama; Hampton Institute in Virginia; Shaw University in North Carolina, and many others.

Early in the twentieth century James B. Duke, the tobacco manufacturer, gave $100 million to Trinity College in North Carolina, which became Duke University. The Carnegie Institute, now Carnegie-Mellon University, opened in Pittsburgh, Pennsylvania in 1905 with a gift from Andrew Carnegie which with additional donations from him and the Carnegie Corporation totalled more than $27 million.

The foregoing includes only a few of the hundreds of philanthropies that provided the basis for the founding of new colleges and universities and nurtured their early development.

After the Second World War

In 1930 there were just over a million students enrolled in colleges and universities; by 1980 this figure had expanded to more than 12 million. Expansion began after the Second World War but grew most rapidly in the 1960s and 1970s, as the following figures show:

1950	2 300 000
1960	3 600 000
1970	8 650 000
1980	12 100 000

After the war some 11 million servicemen returned to civilian life eager to rebuild their lives and begin careers. The Congress had approved the Servicemen's Readjustment Act (commonly known as the GI Bill) in 1944, which provided a stipend and expenses for veterans to attend college and approximately 2.25 million did so, which swelled post-war enrolment rapidly.

Enrolment sagged slightly in the early 1950s, when veterans graduated, but by the mid-fifties it was rising again. In the early 1960s the post-war baby boom began to arrive on campuses, swelling colleges and universities beyond their capacities, and many additional institutions were established.

Much of the expansion in public institutions was absorbed by state colleges and universities that had been converted from teacher's colleges. Most offered the bachelor's degree in a broad range of curricula and the master's degree in many fields. Later a few added doctoral studies in some fields of study. One teacher's college in Wisconsin that enrolled only 500 students in 1953 was a university by 1970, enrolling more than 12 000 students.

Many junior colleges were converted to four-year colleges, and later some became universities offering bachelor's and master's degrees and in some cases PhD degrees. Technical institutes, some of which still retain the technical name, became universities in fact, offering a broad range of degree programmes. In most states by 1980 at least 95 per cent of the population lived within commuting distance of a public four-year or two-year college or university.

Private higher education expanded too. Some small colleges became large universities; however, unlike public institutions which were frequently unable to limit enrolment due to legislative direction, many private colleges, including some of the most distinguished, refused to increase enrolments substantially. They argued that the quality of education offered was dependent on small enrolments with close relationships between faculty and students.

Several private colleges, faced with continuing financial problems, became state institutions by request and some municipally supported colleges also became state institutions.

Student protest

In 1964 at the University of California at Berkeley students initiated protests concerning free speech which soon grew into protests over a variety of issues on other campuses. Much of the protest centred on what students considered to be irrelevant curricula and impersonalization of teaching.

Leading universities were increasingly concentrating on research. In many cases these were public universities that were enrolling growing numbers of students, either by choice or by direction of state legislatures, and much of the undergraduate teaching was being done by teaching assistants, that is, graduate students. Students felt they were being cheated since they attended a particular university to benefit from instruction from outstanding professors but instead were being taught primarily by advanced students.

Most of the protest about curricula and teaching came from students in liberal arts rather than engineering, agriculture, business administration and the other applied fields of study. Students could not relate what they were studying in the arts and sciences to the problems of society.

At the same time there was a rising consciousness concerning the need to integrate blacks into the whole society. The separate-but-equal principle had been declared unconstitutional by the US Supreme Court in 1954 but only limited progress had been made in integrating blacks into schools and colleges. Both black and white students protested and in many cases rioted, damaging buildings and other property on many college campuses.

The Vietnam war also became an issue. Students who wanted to avoid being drafted into the army and possibly to serve in Vietnam initiated sit-ins and demonstrations to protest against the war, some of which led to violence, disruption and damage to property. During this period an organization called Students for a Democratic Society was founded and embarked on a decade of protest and violence that eventually turned not only adults but students against them. The murder of Martin Luther King, the black civil rights leader, in 1968 set off widespread demonstrations, riots and violence.

Student demonstrations and violence peaked in May 1970 when the Vietnam war was extended to bombing the North Vietnamese army in Cambodia. Afterwards there were occasional protests and demonstrations on campuses but from 1970 on they were in decline. The turning point came with the bombing of a classroom building at the University of Wisconsin at Madison in 1971 by radical students who thought that a computer in the building was being used for military research. The reaction among liberal students and faculty who had been tolerant of many of the protests and demonstrations was one of shock and disenchantment with the protest movement. Most students realized that the goals they sought could not be achieved through protest and demonstrations, not to mention violence, and there was growing reaction against such disorders both in colleges and secondary schools; and by the middle of the 1970s students arriving on American college and university campuses were decidedly unsympathetic with those who sought to bring about change through disruption and violence.

While student disorders on campuses attracted a great deal of attention, particularly from television, active participants were decidedly in a minority. Not more than 10 per cent were actively involved in protests and demonstrations and radicals who advocated social revolution and resorted to violence in attempts to achieve it accounted for less than 1 per cent of students.

To what extent student protests influenced changes on American college campuses is not possible to document here but by the 1970s there was clearly a marked change in faculty attitudes towards teaching. Students were receiving more attention and faculty were demonstrating greater concern for teaching. In research and doctoral universities research activity did not diminish but faculty were distinctly focusing more on better teaching, on teaching competence in the awarding of tenure and promotion and other conditions related to student learning. Dozens of institutions began awards programmes to recognize outstanding teaching.

Constitutional issues

One of the most important decisions in American higher education came when the Supreme Court of the United States ruled in 1819 that Dartmouth College was a private, not a public corporation and therefore was free to operate without government interference. The court recognized that private colleges were established in the public interest but that they were not public institutions subject to public control. The court also recognized the board of trustees as the only body legally authorized to act on behalf of the college. This decision had a major influence on the establishment and operation of private colleges in the future and helped to solidify the role of the governing board as the legal spokesman for the institution.

Church-state issues

Before American independence there was little concern about separation of church and state in so far as colleges were concerned, but when the American constitution was written the first amendment specified that the government should take no action to establish an official religion. This continues to be debated today, especially among those who would like to insert prayer or religious teaching into public elementary and secondary schools.

The first amendment has provided the basis for court determinations that no public college or university may offer sectarian religious studies, although non-sectarian religious studies are offered by many public institutions. This has accounted to a considerable extent for the continuing popularity of church-supported colleges among parents who want their children to be educated in a religious environment. While many of the colleges formerly supported by Protestant denominations have become independent, many of them continue to offer religious instruction and provide a religious environment. A sizeable number of colleges continue to provide a highly religious atmosphere for students, especially Catholic supported colleges.

American higher education grew out of the traditions of its European forebears but developed its own patterns and character consonant with a rapidly growing, dynamic, multicultural country. The result is a unique system of higher education as varied in type and quality of institutions as the society it serves. Within three and a half centuries American higher education grew from one religion-oriented college, venerable Harvard, to a complicated network of more than 3000 institutions.

Note

1   Each of the states is divided into counties with county governments. There are 3024 counties in the fifty American states; Delaware and Hawaii, with three counties each, have the smallest number and Texas, with 254, the largest number.

2 Organization and governance

Many visitors to America are perplexed by the variety of institutions of higher education, the terms used to identify them, the inconsistencies in these terms and the titles of institutions' administrators. Some Americans are also unclear about them because of the great diversity that exists in American higher education.

The high degree of autonomy allowed to private institutions from the early days of higher education has resulted in dozens of variations among them alone; the founders or trustees of each shaped the institution to fit their wishes, usually without guidance or direction from government or other external agencies. Since education is a state function and the federal government exercises no influence over the organization of state institutions, in each of the fifty states public colleges and universities were shaped by the state legislatures, governors, higher education governing boards and others involved in their establishment and management.

Colleges, universities and institutes

In some countries the central government requires institutions, public and private, to meet certain requirements to be called a university and others to be called a college. No such regulations exist in the US; thus one finds indiscriminate use of the terms university, college and institute.

Early institutions of higher learning in America were called colleges, a term adopted from England. Most of the institutions established over the next 300 years were, at least in the beginning, single purpose and called colleges. Two-year normal schools, established later to prepare teachers, became four-year teacher's colleges and then state colleges when they added other curricula, mostly after the Second World War.

In the latter end of the nineteenth century when private colleges began to add graduate studies, many of them substituted university for college in the institution's name. As each state established its premier institution it was called institute, seminary, college or similar but soon came to be called university. The land-grant institutions that were separate from the premier universities were all labelled college until the 1950s when, within a few years, all substituted university for college in their names.

Many early institutions specializing in science, engineering and technology were called institutes; most of them have changed to university but some of the nation's leading universities are still called institutes, for example, Massachusetts Institute of Technology, and California Institute of Technology.

A university generally refers to an institution that offers undergraduate degrees in liberal arts and professional fields, plus graduate study in at least one field, usually more than one, and often post-baccalaureate study in one or more professional fields such as medicine, dentistry or law. A few such institutions offer only undergraduate study, plus one post-baccalaureate degree programme, for example, the University of the South in Tennessee which offers postgraduate study in theology. Several private liberal arts colleges offer only the bachelor's degree and are called universities, but as a general rule a university offers graduate study and in many cases postgraduate professional study.

The term college, in referring to higher education, is used in four ways:

1 It refers to an institution with programmes leading to the bachelor's degree, although some colleges offer graduate study, usually leading to the master's degree; a few colleges offer the PhD degree and a few offer postgraduate professional degrees and are universities, in fact if not in name. Dartmouth College in New Hampshire offers master's, PhD and MD degrees, in addition to being one of the leading undergraduate institutions in the country.

2 A unit within a university similar to a faculty in European universities is called a college. In a typical university we find a college of liberal arts or college of arts and sciences which usually includes the humanities, social-behavioural sciences, fine arts, natural sciences and mathematics. Within the university there may also be

a college of engineering, college of business administration, college of education and postgraduate professional programmes such as college of medicine, college of law and college of dentistry.

3   Two-year colleges: some are called junior colleges, some community colleges and others simply colleges. A few are called technical colleges.

4   Finally the term college is used in a generic sense to refer to all higher education. Thus reference to the number of students enrolling in colleges refers to all colleges and universities.

The term college is also used in reference to institutions not classified as higher education. For example, the American College of Surgeons is an association, not an institution of higher education. Schools for training barbers are often called colleges, and the term is also applied to private schools of less than college level engaged in providing other short-term skills training.

Institute, as already noted, was originally used to identify an institution of higher education that specialized in scientific, engineering and technical studies, and many such institutes still exist. In addition as universities developed, particularly after the Second World War, they established internal components called institutes to pursue research on specialized subjects, for example, Institute of Molecular Physics, Social Science Research Institute, Industrial Relations Institute, and dozens more. While most are engaged in research, the term institute has also been adopted in some institutions for components concerned with a wider variety of activities, including service and, in a few cases, teaching.

Also within universities are found centres of many kinds. A centre is likely to be an interdisciplinary unit whose work is not identical with that of a single department and which may be engaged in graduate studies, service activities, research or a combination of all three.

The term school normally refers to elementary and secondary education; however there are exceptions. When an institution of higher education is organized like a university but is titled college, internal components are usually called schools instead of colleges, for example, School of Arts and Sciences, School of Business Administration, and so on. In a few universities the only college is arts and sciences and undergraduate professional components are known as schools. In some private universities there is a college of arts and sciences which offers the only baccalaureate degree programmes awarded by the university and all professional studies are postgraduate and are known as schools. Thus at Harvard the college of arts and sciences (known as Harvard College) offers the only baccalaureate degrees; in addition to the

Graduate School of Arts and Sciences there are several professional schools that require a college degree for admission and award only postgraduate degrees, for instance EdD, MBA, DBA, and others.

Some private single purpose institutions are called schools instead of colleges or universities, for example, School of Law, School of Medicine, School of Fine Arts, plus some two-year schools, especially profit-making institutions.

Institutions classified

The diversity of American higher education becomes more apparent when we examine the nature and extent of differentiation among categories of institutions.

By institutional type

In its studies over a period of years ending in 1980, the Carnegie Council on Policy Studies in Higher Education classified colleges and universities into five types, some of which were further subdivided. The five types and numbers of each are shown in Table 2.1.

Table 2.1

Institutions of higher education by
Carnegie classification, 1977

Carnegie classification	Public	Private	Total
		(number)	
Doctorate granting universities:			
Major research universities	62	36	98
Other doctorate universities	57	29	86
Comprehensive colleges and universities	354	239	593
Liberal arts college:			
Highly selective	0	123	123
Other liberal arts college	11	457	468
Two-year colleges	923	255	1178
Other specialized institutions	75	503	578

Source: *Three Thousand Features*, Final Report of the Carnegie Council on Policy Studies in Higher Education, Jossey-Bass, San Francisco, 1980.

Of the slightly less than 200 doctoral granting universities so classified, almost a hundred were classified as major research universities because they were among the top hundred institutions receiving federal research funding annually and awarded substantial numbers of PhD and comparable degrees, essentially fifty or more per year. Other doctoral universities included those that awarded at least ten doctorates per year in not less than three fields of study. (This excluded specialized institutions that awarded PhD degrees but in only one or two fields.)

The distinction between research universities and other doctoral granting universities does not enjoy total agreement among academics. Some spokesmen in the leading research universities would insist that some of the institutions at the bottom in a rank order of research universities are not in fact major research universities. At the same time some of those in other doctoral granting universities, especially those at the top in rank order, would argue that their institutions are major research universities.

Comprehensive colleges and universities offer the baccalaureate degree in liberal arts (arts and sciences) and in one or more undergraduate professional fields, for example, education, business, engineering and agriculture, plus graduate study leading to the master's degree and sometimes postgraduate professional study. A few of these institutions offer limited doctoral studies, usually in one or two fields, and award a small number of doctoral degrees.

Liberal arts colleges consist essentially of institutions awarding the bachelor's degree in liberal arts; however many of them offer limited undergraduate professional studies. A few offer some graduate study at the master's degree level only, and award a few master's degrees annually.

The Carnegie Council further classified liberal arts colleges into highly selective, which includes about 20 per cent of the group, and non-selective. Most Americans have heard of the highly selective liberal arts colleges but there are almost 500 private liberal arts colleges that are little known beyond their constituencies — the denomination that supports them or the state where they are located — except for a few that gain wide visibility through athletics, for example, winning a national sports championship. Most of these colleges were founded in the nineteenth century, are located in small towns, enrol fewer than 1000 students, have small endowments and must depend primarily on tuition and fees, yet they educate approximately 500 000 students and are an important component of American higher education.

Specialized institutions include a wide variety of undergraduate, graduate and postgraduate professional, largely single purpose institutions. Among them are approximately 200 theological seminaries and Bible colleges, most of them quite small, all private and supported financially by denominations with which they are affiliated.

Other specialized institutions include free-standing degree granting schools or colleges of medicine, dentistry, osteopathy, podiatry, optometry, law, pharmacy, nursing, chiropractic, engineering, business, management, technology, art, design, music, dance, drama, maritime studies, languages, teacher education, and others that do not offer undergraduate liberal arts degrees.

According to the US Department of Education there were approximately 660 institutions in the early 1980s in which the highest degree offered was the master's degree. These included those listed under comprehensive colleges and universities in Table 2.1 plus a few liberal arts colleges and specialized institutions.

The US Department of Education also reported that there were approximately 450 institutions that offered the doctorate; these included, in addition to doctoral granting universities, a few comprehensive colleges and universities but the remainder was accounted for by specialized institutions.

Two-year colleges consist primarily of community and junior colleges. Initially junior colleges offered only the first two years of study found in four-year colleges with the expectation that students would transfer after two years to the latter. During the 1960s and especially in the 1970s, public two-year colleges were asked to accept responsibility for preparing students for occupations not formerly offered in colleges. Some of these vocational-technical programmes lead to no degree although many lead to an Associate in Applied Arts or Associate in Applied Science degree. These programmes are numerous including, for example, automotive mechanics, printing, typing, bookkeeping, computer programming, computer repair, welding, sheet metal work, food preparation and service, drafting, horology, and many more.

By 1980 students studying vocational-technical subjects accounted for half the enrolment in public two-year colleges. At the same time a growing number of students were enrolling in programmes for general education who did not plan to transfer to a senior (four-year) college or university. Because of this diversification in programme offerings and increased attention to community needs, many junior colleges were renamed community colleges; most public two-year colleges consider themselves community colleges even though community may not be in their names.

Between 1970 and 1980 enrolment in community/junior colleges doubled — from 2.2 million to 4.4 million — mostly in vocational-technical programmes. While enrolment in academic courses did not decrease in number, as a percentage of total enrolment the decline was sharp.

Some private two-year colleges continue to offer only academic programmes for students who plan to transfer to senior colleges and universities and still identify themselves as junior colleges; several are for women only.

Of the private two-year colleges shown in Table 2.1 some are profit-making technical institutes that provide little or no general education. The US Department of Education reported that in 1982–3 there were 3280 institutions of higher education in the country. The creation of new four-year degree granting colleges and universities virtually ended in the mid-1970s, hence the difference is accounted for largely by two-year colleges. Of the additional 156, compared with the list in Table 2.1, 97 were two-year colleges and of this number 80 were private, mostly profit-making technical colleges or institutes. The remainder were largely specialized institutions. Any increase in the number of institutions of higher education before the year 2000 is likely to be primarily private, proprietary technical colleges and secondarily specialized degree granting institutions, some of which will also be proprietary.

In addition to the foregoing there are other non-degree granting institutions that are not considered higher education but are sometimes included under the broad category of post-secondary education. Most do not require secondary school education for admission and offer programmes of widely varying duration — from a few weeks to two years. Among these are trade and technical institutions, usually called schools but occasionally colleges, that prepare students for both blue collar and white collar occupations.

Almost all these schools are profit-making enterprises. No one has identified them all partly because some of them operate for brief periods; by one estimate there are 8000 such schools in the country but this is probably conservative. They offer training for barbers, beauticians, bartenders, radio and television broadcasting and equipment repair, other electronics, medical and dental technicians, court reporting, secretaries, construction, computer programmers and pilots. They also provide training in bookkeeping and other business studies, tourism, hotel management, automobile driving, fencing, computer repair, languages and many more.

These private schools offer many of the same programmes offered by community colleges, usually at greater cost; however they enrol large numbers of students, primarily because they promise to prepare them more quickly for employment, and often because of elaborate advertising. Some are well established with outstanding reputations for quality education, while many are opened with inadequate capital, provide inferior training and last only a short time, closing for lack of capital, lack of students or to avoid legal prosecution.

By sex

The first college for women was Troy Female Seminary in New York which was established in 1821, and the first college to admit both men and women was Oberlin College, Ohio, when it was established in 1833. Among institutions established during the latter part of the nineteenth century, almost all the public institutions and most of the private colleges admitted both sexes but a number of single-sex colleges were created. The creation of single-sex colleges continued until the 1960s when, in 1963–4, the number peaked at 519 of which 240 were for men and 279 for women.

In the 1960s women began to insist on admission to several leading men's colleges, many of whose alumni fervently opposed their admission, but before long Harvard, Yale and many other men's colleges admitted women and later many women's colleges admitted men. By 1981–2 there were only 215 single-sex colleges, 104 for men and 111 for women, but of the 215 only 139 were degree granting institutions – 57 for men and 82 for women. Of the remaining 76, 27 were two-year colleges and 49 were non-degree institutions, principally engaged in training rabbis and priests.

The 1980s saw a rejuvenation of women's colleges. From 1975 to 1985 enrolment in women's colleges grew by 25 per cent. Several factors were involved including marked changes in some of the women's colleges. Some of them developed programmes especially for mature women who wanted to return to college to prepare for different jobs or had reared children and sought something interesting to do. Women's colleges, long confined largely to the liberal arts, began to add business and technical curricula and to increase their emphasis on science. And some women students who had seen women's colleges as anathema to women's liberation decided that the opposite was the case, that they could achieve their fullest potential in single-sex institutions as well as or better than in co-ed institutions.

Federal institutions

The federal government operates many civilian and military training programmes and schools but only ten military institutions award academic degrees. These include officer training academies for the army, navy, air force, coast guard and merchant marine, all of which award the baccalaureate degree. In addition the air force, navy and army operate postgraduate institutions leading to graduate degrees only. The Uniformed Services University of the Health Sciences trains physicians for all the services. The Community College of the Air Force, with branches on many air force bases, provides training primarily civilian in nature but includes many programmes of technical

22

studies of value to the air force; all its programmes are of two years duration or less and several lead to associate degrees.

The federal government also supports three community colleges for American Indians plus Howard University in Washington, DC, created after the Civil War for blacks, and Gallaudet College for the deaf, also in Washington, DC.

Early in the history of the country there was an effort to establish a national university under federal auspices but the Congress has continually opposed it partly owing to the constitutional basis that education is the responsibility of the states and partly to the historical role of private higher education in America.

Public vs. private

Private higher education has dominated in America from its beginning and continues to do so in terms of the number of institutions but not in enrolments. In 1950–1 there were 1859 institutions of higher education of which 638 were public and 1221 private. Thirty years later there were 3270 institutions – 1510 public and 1760 private. Most of the increase occurred between 1960 and 1980 – from 2040 in 1960 to 3270 in 1980, an increase of 60 per cent.

Between 1950 and 1980 total enrolment grew from 2.3 million to 12 million. In 1950 private colleges and universities enrolled 50 per cent of the students; by 1980 they enrolled only 22 per cent.

The decline in percentage of students enrolled in private institutions can be misleading. In actual numbers the enrolment in private institutions increased – from 1.14 million in 1950 to 2.66 million in 1980, an increase of 133 per cent. But during the same period enrolment in public institutions increased more than 700 per cent.

There are several reasons for the shift from private to public higher education. A major factor was the establishment of several hundred community colleges, which for the most part served students who could not afford to attend college unless there was one in their home town. A second factor was the increase in public degree granting institutions, especially in the eastern part of the US which historically had relied largely on private colleges and universities. In response to the demand for higher education New Jersey, New York, Pennsylvania, Massachusetts, and other eastern states that had lagged in the development of public higher education, established many new colleges and universities and expanded teacher's colleges into comprehensive colleges and universities.

A third factor was cost; private higher education, particularly the more selective colleges and universities, became very expensive compared with public institutions. Many students who would have preferred to attend private colleges or universities found it necessary, financially, to attend state supported institutions. Finally there was a large increase in minorities, particularly blacks, attending college, and most of them attended public institutions.

Private colleges are generally smaller than public institutions. In 1983 some 60 per cent of the private colleges enrolled fewer than 1000 students each, and 86 per cent enrolled fewer than 2500 each. But only 10 per cent of the public institutions enrolled fewer than 1000 students and 37 per cent enrolled fewer than 2500 students. Thirty-one institutions enrolled more than 30 000 students each, of which two were private and twenty-nine public.

Private institutions include those affiliated with religious groups, of which more than 200 are identified with the Roman Catholic church and more than 500 with various Protestant denominations, plus 34 with other religions. Also included are more than 800 colleges and universities that are independent and not affiliated to any religious denomination. Finally there are more than 150 colleges organized as profit-making institutions, most of which are specialized two-year institutions.

Of the 800 or so independent colleges and universities a considerable number began with church support but are no longer affiliated to a denomination. In many cases the denomination withdrew financial support, prompting the institutions to terminate church affiliation. In others, colleges terminated the affiliation in order to participate in the Teachers' Insurance and Annuity Association, a foundation-sponsored pension programme for college teachers.

In a strict sense the term independent college refers to a private college that has no religious or church affiliation but the term is often used interchangeably with private college or to indicate all non-government higher education institutions.

Private institutions, including church affiliated, independent and proprietary, are so categorized because their governance is not control-led by a government agency and their financing is not the responsibility of a governmental agency, although many private institutions receive government funds and students in most of them receive financial aid from federal and/or state governments.

Regulation of private institutions by state governments is minimal for the most part — only when federal or state tax funds are involved and not in respect of courses offered, degrees awarded, salaries paid, instruction, or other aspects of the institution's teaching, research and service. If a private institution or its students receive federal or state funds the institution must account to the source of funds concerning how they are spent. When faculty in private institutions receive federal or state government research grants or contracts, their institutions are also accountable for the expenditure of those funds and for obeying affirmative action and equal employment laws and regulations. Bogus institutions are subject to prosecution for misleading the public but legitimate academic institutions are relatively free of governmental regulation.

State systems

There are many variations between the states in their organization of higher education but they also have much in common. Each state has a premier university, sometimes called flagship university, that serves the entire state and offers doctoral degrees. In twenty-nine states it is also the land-grant university, which means that it offers agriculture; all the premier state universities except Indiana University offer engineering. In twenty states there is a separate land-grant university that originally specialized in agriculture and engineering but which, in recent years, added colleges of business administration, education, arts and sciences, and others normally found in a university with broad curricular offerings, although most do not offer medicine, dentistry, law or pharmacy.

In a few states, in addition to the premier state university and the land-grant university, there are one or more doctoral granting universities which are only slightly behind the premier university on several measures. For example, within the University of California system, close behind the premier University of California at Berkeley is the University of California at Los Angeles, one of the top ten research universities in the country; in addition to the land-grant university at Davis and the health science university and law school in San Francisco there are five major universities, all established since the Second World War, that have noteworthy graduate programmes.

In each of the states of Florida and Arizona there is a second university that is considered equal to the premier university in many of its programmes. In the state of New York, in addition to state colleges and community colleges and the City University of New York, all public, there are four doctoral granting state universities, none of which has been designated as the state's flagship university.

Comprehensive state colleges and universities constitute the largest group of public degree granting institutions. Although they all admit students from towns throughout their own state and from other states and countries, each enrol students primarily from its local region. Every state has one or more such institution except Wyoming, a sparsely populated state, which has only one university and seven community colleges.

In California, in addition to the University of California system with ten universities, there is another state system known as the California State University System which consists of nineteen comprehensive state colleges and universities. All nineteen offer bachelor's and master's degrees and some post-master's study towards the PhD degree which can be completed at one of the universities in the University of California system.

As noted in Chapter 1, most comprehensive state colleges and universities were established late in the last century or early in the twentieth century as two-year normal schools to train public school teachers. During the 1920s and 1930s most were changed to four-year teacher's colleges and in the 1950s and 1960s to state colleges offering not only teacher education but also bachelor's and master's degrees in liberal arts, business administration and, in some of them, agriculture, home economics, engineering and other fields of study. In the 1960s and 1970s most of these institutions were renamed universities; only a small number continue to be called colleges. A few offer Doctor of Education programmes and fewer still offer the PhD degree in limited fields of study.

Baccalaureate institutions are in the minority among public institutions; usually they are single purpose or limited purpose institutions. The large majority of liberal arts colleges are private.

Most specialized institutions are also found in the private sector; however there are some in this category (Table 2.1) such as free-standing medical schools, law schools, art schools and the like, that are public.

Community colleges constitute the largest number of public institutions (63 per cent) and enrol approximately 45 per cent of public higher education students. Approximately 40 per cent of the public community colleges are state institutions, financed and governed from the state level. Another 40 per cent are financed jointly by the state government and from local taxes, most of which have a locally elected board of trustees; the remaining 20 per cent are financed solely by local taxes — city, county or local community college taxing district — and have a locally elected board of trustees.

Statewide coordination

During the 1950s state legislatures, boards of trustees and presidents of state colleges and universities began to recognize that with the growing number of institutions in each state, rapidly expanding enrolments and potential for conflict and inefficiencies, coordination of all higher education was needed in each state. Some states had only a single board for all institutions but most did not.

The first step was an attempt at voluntary coordination in which presidents of state colleges and universities met periodically to attempt to reach voluntary agreement on conflicting issues. This eventually proved unworkable.

Soon three types of statewide coordination developed: advisory, regulatory and consolidated governing boards. Advisory coordinating boards have little authority; their main purpose is to advise the legislature and governor of the state concerning matters affecting higher education but they have no power to overrule the boards of trustees of state colleges and universities. This type of coordination is found in eight states.

Regulatory coordinating boards have final authority regarding new degree programmes, major construction, and certain other functions that vary from state to state, but in each case these boards cannot overrule institutional governing boards on some areas of responsibility. Nineteen states have regulatory boards; however the limits of their authority vary. For example, in Ohio the board has final authority over institutional appropriations requests made to the state legislature; in Texas the board does not.

Finally twenty-two states have a single governing board for all senior colleges and universities in the state. In several states institutions have established local advisory boards and the state governing board has delegated limited authority to them. One state has no statewide co-ordinating or governing board.

The coordinating board in each state has a staff which collects statistics on higher education in the state, prepares recommendations for the board and works with state colleges and universities to carry out policies established by the board. The head of the coordinating board staff is styled commissioner in some states, chancellor in others, executive director in some, executive secretary in a few and other titles in the remaining states.

Several states have one statewide coordinating board for senior colleges and universities and another for community-junior colleges.

Institutional systems

Within several states there are systems each consisting of several institutions under a single governing board. Some examples will illustrate: California has three state boards in addition to a statewide coordinating agency; one board for the University of California system (ten universities), a board for the California State University System (nineteen colleges and universities) and a board for the public community college system (106 community colleges). In addition each community college has a local board of trustees that may be responsible for a single college or, as in the case of Los Angeles, one local board for ten community colleges.

In Florida all the nine state universities are part of the State

University System of Florida, with a single governing board. Under the State Board of Education, which is concerned primarily with elementary and secondary schools, is a State Board of Community Colleges that governs the junior colleges each of which also has a local board of trustees.

In the state of Illinois the University of Illinois (three universities) constitutes one system, three other universities constitute a second system, another system includes five other universities and the fourth system consists of two universities; each system has a governing board whose actions are subject to review by the Illinois Board of Higher Education.

The City University of New York includes eighteen institutions — seven community colleges, ten four-year colleges and universities plus a graduate centre granting doctoral degrees. Formerly financed solely by the City of New York, it now receives part of its support from the state government.

In Texas, which has a regulatory coordinating board, there is a combination of governing arrangements. The University of Texas System (fourteen institutions) is governed by one board; there are two systems with four universities in each; three other systems each have three universities; each of the remaining universities has a separate board. Each of the sixty community or junior colleges in the state has a locally elected board or board responsible for two or more community colleges in one district, for example, the Dallas County Community College district includes seven community colleges governed by one board. All these are subject to review by the Co-ordinating Board, Texas State College and University System.

Governing boards

Except for some colleges sponsored by the Catholic church which report directly to a church official, virtually all colleges and universities in the US are governed by a board of trustees composed primarily of laymen. In public institutions it is often called board of regents. A few institutions have a board of trustees that governs the institution plus a board of visitors that serves as an advisory and support group.

The American pattern of governance of higher education began with the establishment of Harvard College. The charter from the government of the colony of Massachusetts states that there must be a board of overseers composed of individuals from outside the college. This pattern has been followed in the founding of most colleges and universities in the US. While different titles for boards are used — overseers, visitors, trustees, regents, supervisors, directors — they are all composed primarily of persons from outside the institution charged with the responsibility of directing the affairs of the college or university.

Boards of trustees for public and private institutions are much alike. The board is the legal body responsible for the institution; the courts regard board actions as official actions of the institution and boards are presumed to have total authority although they delegate much of it to administrators and faculty. In most private institutions title to college property is held in the name of the board. The board serves as court of last resort within the institution.

The board establishes policies for administrators and faculty to follow in operating the institution. It reviews and acts on recommendations by the institution's administration, faculty and students. The board establishes the mission of the institution and is responsible for seeing that it is accomplished. The board approves all purchases and sales of real estate and other major items of property and generally reviews all major decisions made by the administration. It reviews and approves budgets, including salaries, benefits and working conditions. The board chooses the president but usually delegates the hiring of other officers, faculty and staff to the president, subject to board review which in most cases is pro forma.

There are however significant differences between boards of public and private institutions. Boards of public institutions are usually much smaller, ranging in size from five to twenty-five members and averaging nine. Private institution boards are commonly much larger, up to fifty or sixty members and averaging twenty-eight members.

The use of governing boards composed of laymen is based on the proposition that laymen will be more likely to represent the public interest than boards composed of persons who would benefit from board decisions. Although they are not expert managers of colleges and universities, well chosen laymen should be able to make sound judgments based on recommendations of faculty, administrators and others.

Faculty members frequently serve on governing boards but more often in institutions in which they are not employed since to serve on boards of their own institutions would result in conflict of interest. In most private institutions the president is required to be a voting member of the institution's board of trustees but this is rare in public institutions. Many higher education authorities do not recommend that presidents serve as voting members since on small boards, which are common in the public sector, the president is inevitably placed in conflict with board members. The problem is less serious in private institutions whose boards are usually large and the president is less likely to be required to break tie votes on critical issues.

Most institutions aspire to have boards composed of leading citizens, especially those in business and the professions and, in the case of independent institutions, representatives of their constituencies. A survey in 1985 found that business executives accounted for 37 per cent of the membership of boards in both public and private institutions (*CHE*, 12 February 1986). College teachers accounted for 3.5 per cent in private institutions but only 0.9 per cent in public institutions and college administrators another 3.2 per cent and 1.3 per cent respectively. On public institution boards attorneys or judges made up 10.4 per cent but only 5.9 per cent in private institutions; the difference probably reflects the role of politics in appointment of trustees to boards of public institutions. A major difference was found in the percentage of clergy serving as board members — 1 per cent in public institutions and 14.3 per cent in private institutions. Many church-related colleges have church officials serving ex-officio on their boards and some include clergy as a way of communicating with the constituencies the colleges especially wish to serve. Retired persons constituted 11.9 per cent on public institution boards and 9.3 per cent on private institution boards. Among retired persons serving on boards were a higher proportion of educators, especially on public institution boards, and a lower proportion of businessmen, compared with non-retired members.

Trustees of both public and private institutions serve without compensation, and in private institutions they pay their own expenses of attending board meetings and other board business. Many trustees devote a considerable amount of time to these affairs, which for physicians, lawyers, accountants and other professional people in private practice results in a significant reduction in their earnings. None the less few institutions encounter much difficulty in persuading prominent citizens to accept appointments to the board of trustees of a college or university. In most cases trustees are graduates of the college or university and serve because of personal feelings towards the institution. Others want to contribute to public service and find service as a trustee satisfying and sometimes professionally rewarding.

Much of the work of boards is done by trustee committees. A typical board will have committees concerned with academic affairs, student affairs, personnel, finance, investment, buildings and grounds, health affairs if the institution has a medical school, and an executive committee which is empowered to act on matters that cannot wait for scheduled meetings.

Beginning in the 1960s public and private institutions initiated efforts to increase the number of women and minorities on boards of trustees. By 1985 women accounted for 19.6 per cent of the trustees in private institutions and 23.1 per cent in public institutions; blacks made up 5.5 per cent of the membership on private institution boards and 11.4 per cent on boards of public institutions, the latter almost equal to the percentage of blacks in the total population. Both public and private institutions continue to increase the proportion of women and minorities on their boards of trustees; more recently greater effort has been made to increase the proportion of Hispanics on boards.

Public institutions

In most states trustees for boards of state colleges and universities are nominated by the governor of the state, subject to approval by the state senate. In five states trustees are elected by popular vote. In several states some of the members of each board are designated — representatives of labour organizations, farmers, industry, government officials, alumni and students. They are either selected by their constituencies for such service or serve because they are officers of their respective organizations.

In several states members of the executive branch serve ex-officio as members of one or more governing boards, for example, in Alabama the governor is chairman of the board of the land-grant university. In Florida the state commissioner of elementary and secondary education is an ex-officio member of the board of regents of the State University System. In the state of Colorado, the State Board of Agriculture also serves as the governing board of Colorado State University, the land-grant institution.

The method of selecting trustees is continually debated. Trustees appointed by state governors are often outstanding but are sometimes nominated primarily because of their service to the political party or the governor's election campaign. Governors generally try to appoint qualified people not only because of the wish to ensure sound management of state colleges and universities but also to avoid the embarrassment that could result from the appointment of a trustee who performed poorly.

Trustees for about 60 per cent of the public community colleges are chosen by popular vote locally, and since most community college districts correspond to a town, city or county the candidates and their qualifications are likely to be known to the voters. Most community colleges receive at least part of their income from local taxes, and campaigns for trustee positions are often quite spirited. In those states where public community colleges are state institutions trustees are appointed by the governor and/or other public officials.

The most common length of term for trustees in public colleges and universities is six years, with 60 per cent serving six-year terms or longer although four-year terms are also common. In a few cases terms are as much as ten to twelve years and in one state sixteen years, established by the legislature to prevent any governor of that state from appointing during his term of office a majority of trustees for an institution. Reappointment of trustees in public institutions is less common than in private institutions, particularly in states where governors of different political parties are elected alternately. Student trustees usually serve one-year terms. Ex-officio members serve as long as they are in office in the organization they represent or as long as their constituency continues to elect or appoint them.

Boards of many public four-year colleges and universities meet six times per year but almost as many meet only four times a year, and a few meet monthly. Although most trustees agree that their role should be limited to policy making with administration left to the institutions' administrators, frequency of meetings and geographical proximity to the institution affect the extent of trustee involvement in administrative decisions. Hence community college boards, all of whose members typically live in the community where the college is located and meet monthly, tend to become more involved in administrative decisions than other boards.

Private institutions

Boards of trustees in most private colleges and universities are self-perpetuating, that is, the current board selects future board members. Although terms of office may be shorter than those in public institutions, usually three or four years, most trustees in private institutions are re-elected to several terms. In most private institutions the board of trustees has a nominating committee that is responsible for locating new potential trustees and for recommending non-reappointment of trustees whose service to the institution and its board is lacking.

Unfortunately some committees and boards are reluctant to terminate nonproductive trustees and allow them to continue as members when they should be terminated. It is not unusual for trustees of private institutions to serve until they die. By the mid-1980s some boards appeared to have recognized the seriousness of the problem and were taking steps to limit the number of consecutive years a trustee could serve.

In approximately 13 per cent of the private four-year colleges trustees are appointed by church officials. Some Catholic colleges do not have boards of trustees; the president reports directly to church officials. In other cases the colleges have governing boards composed entirely or primarily of church officials; in these cases there is a growing tendency for the college to have an additional advisory board of laymen.

Most boards of private institutions meet three or four times a year; in a few institutions boards meet only once or twice a year but empower the executive committee, which meets more frequently, to act on most matters. The latter occurs most often when boards are large — fifty or more members — and members are scattered over several states.

Trustees of private institutions not only meet less frequently, on average, than those in public institutions but must devote much of their time to the task of fund raising, hence such boards tend to delegate more administrative decisions to the institution's officers.

Most individuals who serve as trustees of private colleges and universities support the institutions financially or are successful in persuading others to do so. Some private institutions have a separate board for the institution's foundation which solicits gifts but most private institutions rely on the governing board to solicit financial gifts.

Internal structure

American colleges and universities are structured more like the corporate model than most European universities yet the structure can be deceiving. Power and influence are generally much more diffused than an organization chart would suggest.

The internal structure of public and private institutions is basically the same; the main differences are between types of institution rather than whether they are in public or private control.

Figure 2.1 shows a typical organizational chart for a large research university. The president is assisted by several vice presidents, each of whom has responsibility for a segment of university activity.

Undergraduate colleges and schools

Academic departments are clustered into colleges or schools. There is wide variation in placement of disciplines and departments. Typically all the basic arts and science disciplines are located in a college of arts and sciences or college of liberal arts, as shown in Figure 2.2. However in some very large universities the arts and sciences are found in four colleges: college of humanities, college of social sciences, college of natural sciences (including mathematics), and college of fine arts. The psychology department is usually located with the social sciences, sometimes called social-behavioural sciences, but in former teacher's colleges psychology is sometimes located in the college of education.

Undergraduate professional programmes such as architecture, social work, library science, pharmacy, nursing and journalism are sometimes departments within colleges but more commonly they are colleges or schools headed by a dean, partly on the insistence of accrediting associations for those fields.

When not a separate college or school architecture is usually a

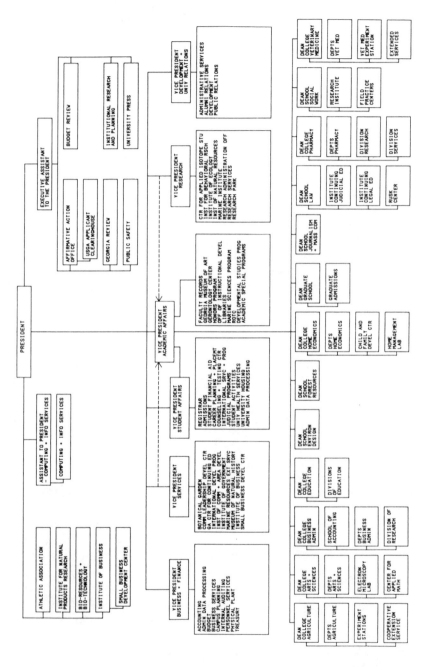

Figure 2.1 Administrative Organization of the University of Georgia

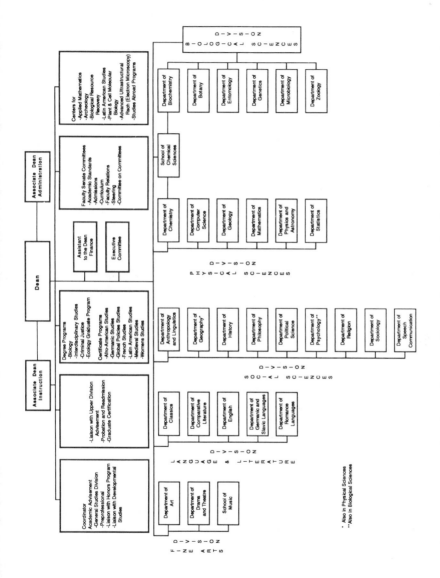

Figure 2.2 Organization of the College of Arts and Sciences, University of Georgia

department in a college of engineering, a college of design or a college of fine arts. Journalism, when it is a department and there is no college of communications, is usually found in the college of arts and sciences but is occasionally found in the college of business administration. Plant pathology is a component of botany, but in land-grant universities it may be a separate department in the college of agriculture. Veterinary medicine is usually a department in the college of agriculture until it begins to award the DVM degree at which time it becomes a separate college with a dean.

Courses in public administration are usually taught in a department of political science or government unless the institution wishes to emphasize that area of study, in which case it usually creates a school of public administration headed by a dean. Physical education is a department in a college of education at many institutions but in others it is a separate college that also includes a department of health education, a department of recreation administration and sometimes a department of dance, although dance is more often found with the performing arts or fine arts.

Terminology varies considerably among institutions. For example, the department of sociology is sometimes known as department of social relations. Geology may appear in departments of geology, geological sciences, or earth sciences. Biology is called life sciences in some institutions. Computer science is usually a department with the natural sciences but sometimes with engineering; the hardware aspects of computer science may be a part of the department of electrical engineering.

The foregoing structure of colleges or schools within institutions is found largely in universities. Private liberal arts colleges have no administrative unit between the department and the central administration, primarily owing to size and also to their single purpose; neither have community colleges. Many specialized institutions are organized like universities with schools, usually not called colleges, composed of academic departments, but a large percentage have no intermediate administrative unit between departments and the central administration. In some single purpose institutions there are no departments.

In a small liberal arts or comprehensive college, which may have only two or three faculty members in some fields of study, combinations of disciplines into departments are common, for example, department of history and political science; department of natural sciences (physics, chemistry, biology, and geology); department of fine arts (art, music, drama and possibly dance); a department of literature and languages.

Academic departments

In colleges and universities that have academic departments, and this

36

includes all universities and most colleges, the department is the organizational unit in which teaching and research takes place. As noted earlier, in small institutions several related disciplines may be combined into one department; on the other hand in large universities and in highly specialized institutions such as medical schools, disciplines may be subdivided into two or more departments.

Figure 2.2 presents a typical departmental organization for a college of arts and sciences in a large university. In a smaller university anthropology would probably be combined with sociology; genetics, botany, microbiology and zoology would be combined into a department of biological sciences, and entomology would be in agriculture.

Faculty appointments are in departments, their tenure is identified with a department, students identify with departments, courses are offered by departments and departments are responsible for providing degree programmes for both undergraduate and graduate students.

In non-departmentalized schools such as schools of architecture, law, public administration and others, the school functions as both a department and a college.

The academic department is so basic to the academic enterprise that it seems to survive most attempts at reorganization or restructuring. The department has been highly criticized because it tends to foster specialization and makes a broad undergraduate education more difficult. A constant complaint of administrators is that there are high walls between departments, that they do not know what others are doing and are not influenced by other departments. Departments, especially in large research universities, are often accused of operating as if they are autonomous units attached to the university for services.

Many approaches have been attempted to lower walls between departments, to foster interdepartmental study and to improve communication among departments. Interdisciplinary degree programmes is one example; research institutes involving faculty from several departments is another. In some institutions loosely assembled divisions have been established consisting of several disciplines or related specialities; invariably faculty within a discipline or field of study join together informally to coordinate their work, providing further justification for the academic department.

Graduate education

With the exception of a few universities the administration of undergraduate and graduate education are separate. The academic department is responsible for both but reports to the graduate school office concerning graduate education matters — programmes, students, standards and certification of those who are to receive graduate degrees. Not all faculty are approved to teach in graduate programmes; within

37

an academic department, particularly one with large freshman course enrolments, there will be several faculty not approved for one or more reasons — they do not hold the doctorate, teach no graduate courses, direct no graduate student research, lack research productivity, and others.

Policies of graduate schools and approval of graduate faculty are usually under the direction of a graduate council composed of elected members of the graduate faculty. A few of the leading doctoral granting research universities have eliminated the graduate faculty designation because almost all their faculty members hold the doctorate or other appropriate terminal degree.

Postgraduate professional education

Postgraduate professional schools or colleges, such as medicine, dentistry and law, requiring those admitted to hold a baccalaureate degree, fit into the university structure in the same way as undergraduate colleges. However in very large universities with comprehensive programmes in the health sciences, those colleges and schools may be under the direction of a vice president for health sciences instead of the vice president for academic affairs. When the university is located in a town or small city its health sciences programmes are likely to be located elsewhere in a large city where there are adequate numbers of patients for clinical training.

Programmes of study in several professional fields, for example, business administration, education, social work, library science, public administration and journalism, are offered at both the undergraduate and postgraduate levels in some universities but, as previously noted, in a few, principally private universities, only programmes in the arts and sciences are offered at the undergraduate level and all professional studies are offered at the postgraduate level only.

The PhD, MA and MS degree programmes are always under the direction of the graduate school because they are, or were originally intended to be, research degrees. In most universities graduate degree programmes in most professional fields — business administration (MBA and DBA), education (MEd and EdD), social work (MSW and DSW), public administration (MPA and DPA) and others — are also under the direction of the graduate school, but in some universities those programmes are not the responsibility of the graduate school. They are solely under the direction of the college or school faculty and administration, as is always the case in medicine (MD), dentistry (DDS or DMD) and law (JD), on the basis that they are professional practice, not research, degrees. However, as explained below (p. 91), the distinction between PhD programmes and some professional

38

practice programmes leading to the doctorate, for example, EdD and DBA, is often imprecise.

Compared with many countries American higher education lacks tidiness in structure and governance. It consists of a multiplicity of types of institution ranging from those concentrating on classical studies to some whose claim to being *higher* education is questionable. Although public institutions serve almost 80 per cent of the students, a majority of the institutions are private and strive to limit governmental intervention.

With few exceptions the governance of American colleges and universities follows a common pattern. The board of trustees is standard and its role is commonly understood by academicians everywhere.

3 Administration and finance

To many academicians the ideal university is a community of scholars supported by a small, largely unseen staff who unobtrusively keep the institution and its services operating. Such a romanticized situation is scarcely to be found in any American college or university today.

One leading state university in the mid-1980s had on one campus 48 000 students, 2200 faculty, 2000 part-time teaching and research personnel (mostly graduate students), 1400 academic and student assistants, 150 librarians, 700 administrators and 10 500 support staff: a total of 16 950 employees. Within the university were sixteen colleges and schools, fifty-four academic departments and 253 undergraduate and graduate degree programmes offering 6300 courses. The operating budget, including income from student fees, food and housing, sales and services, state appropriations, research grants and contacts and other income, totalled almost $500 million. The campus consisted of 300 acres (121 hectares) on which were located 110 buildings. However this university was one of the three largest on a single campus in the country and was atypical.

A more typical situation, a comprehensive university with 10 000 students, would have approximately 500 faculty members, would rely far less on part-time faculty and graduate student teaching assistants and would have fewer non-academic staff proportional to enrolment than the large university.

Except for small colleges the financing and administration of American colleges and universities have become major enterprises requiring the talents of hundreds, if not thousands, of staff in each institution in addition to faculty, and budgets totalling many millions of dollars.

Administrative officers

The earliest colleges in America consisted of a few teachers and a president who was also a teacher. The president usually had two assistants — one who handled day-to-day duties of a business nature and cared for the buildings plus a secretary who served as registrar.

Today a typical university will have a minimum of three vice presidents, often more, thirty to fifty directors of administrative and service units, and a dean for each academic college with one or more assistant and/or associate deans in each.

Generally private colleges and universities, except for the most impecunious, have more support staff personnel proportionately than public institutions. Private institutions devote more resources to the admissions function — visiting secondary schools seeking talented students and providing scholarships for them. They also have larger development staffs since they are more dependent on private giving. For example, a state university with 20 000 students would typically have one development officer and one secretary. A private college with 3000 students might have, in addition to a chief development officer, three or four assistants plus two or three clerks and secretaries.

The president

The president (called chancellor in some institutions) of an American college or university is responsible for the total institution. A president is expected to be fully knowledgeable about academic affairs, an astute financial manager, a good public speaker, skilful in public relations and a master in personal relations. Although informed citizens know the president cannot personally know everything that goes on in the institution, they are often disappointed if he does not.

Perhaps the best brief description of the job of an American university president was given by Clark Kerr, when he was president of the University of California (1963):

> The university president in the United States is expected to be a friend of the students, a colleague of the faculty, a good fellow with the alumni, a sound administrator with the trustees, a good speaker with the public, an astute bargainer with the foundations and the federal agencies, a politician with the state legislature, a friend of industry, labor, and agriculture, a persuasive diplomat with donors, a champion of education generally, a supporter of the professions (particularly law and medicine), a spokesman to the press, a scholar in his own right, a public servant at the state and national levels, a devotee of opera and football equally, a decent human being, a good husband and father, an active member

of a church. Above all he must enjoy traveling in airplanes, eating his meals in public, and attending public ceremonies. No one can be all of these things. Some succeed at being none.

He should be firm, yet gentle; sensitive to others, insensitive to himself; look to the past and the future, yet be firmly planted in the present; both visionary and sound; affable, yet reflective; know the value of a dollar and realize that ideas cannot be bought; inspiring in his visions yet cautious in what he does; a man of principle yet able to make a deal; a man with broad perspective who will follow the details conscientiously; a good American but ready to criticize the status quo fearlessly; a seeker of truth where the truth may not hurt too much; a source of public policy pronouncements when they do not reflect on his own institution. He should sound like a mouse at home and look like a lion abroad. He is one of the marginal men in a democratic society — of whom there are many others — on the margin of many groups, many ideas, many endeavors, many characteristics. He is a marginal man but at the very center of the total process.

The president is assisted by a staff, often a large one in a major institution, but donors, major government officials, legislators, business leaders and often parents of students insist on talking with the president rather than a staff member who might know more about the matter of concern.

Even though some of them are well compensated, most college and university presidents could earn much more in the business world. Every year several depart for leadership positions in business, government and foundations, some at twice or three times their university salaries; but most remain in academe. When asked why the typical answer centres on the opportunity to shape programmes and to serve society in a way that they find highly satisfying. Most presidents and other academic administrators continue to consider themselves academic professionals rather than primarily administrators and most administrators return to teaching and research after a period in administration.

A major function of the president is to legitimize actions proposed by various components of the institution, which usually involves approving or vetoing recommendations from students, faculty or other administrators. The president is expected to see the total picture and to be able to judge whether a given course of action, which might be highly desirable for one sector of the institution, would impinge on the legitimate rights of another part of the university, a law, policy or outside interests.

Until well after the Second World War presidents of most American colleges and universities enjoyed considerable autonomy in the management of their institutions and consulted minimally with faculty and other constituencies, other than their boards of trustees. By 1970 that had changed almost completely. Successful presidents consulted frequently with faculty, students, legislators, alumni and others, in addition to their boards.

The role of a college or university president is to a considerable extent like that of a mayor of a city. He may have a great deal of authority but must use it sparingly. Most of the time he must persuade and lead people in the direction desired. It is true that the president is a gatekeeper in that he makes many final decisions. As the representative of the board of trustees the president must be able to judge how the board will respond to a given problem or else be talented enough to persuade the board to accept his recommended course of action.

College and university presidents come from a variety of backgrounds. A majority of them come through academic channels, hold earned degrees and have been faculty members and administrators in academic institutions. Most of them have been vice presidents or deans although occasionally a president comes directly from a department chairmanship or directorship. Traditionally the president was most likely to have been vice president for academic affairs but as institutions increasingly face financial problems boards of trustees have appointed vice presidents of business or financial affairs to the presidency. They also look outside academe and name as president former government officials, business leaders, foundation executives and others, although academics continue to predominate. Some presidents who do not have an academic background have difficulty adjusting to the academic culture and the autonomy enjoyed by faculty and remain in the position only briefly.

Until recent years the only women presidents were found in colleges for women, but in 1984, 294 or almost 10 per cent of the college and university presidents were women.

Chief academic officer

This position is usually titled vice president for academic affairs; however in a small college it may be called dean of the college or dean of faculty. In a few institutions it is called provost, indicating that the occupant is not only responsible for academic affairs but is the senior officer under the president and is automatically in charge of the institution in the absence of the president.

The chief academic officer is responsible for all activities relating to teaching, research and most of the institution's service activities — all the colleges and schools including the graduate school, academic centres and institutes, libraries, research laboratories, and in some institutions museums, registrar's office, computer services, teaching hospitals and clinics, and others.

The chief academic officer is responsible for curricula, instruction, selection and appointment of faculty, faculty morale, academic quality and other aspects of the institution's academic activities although in each case direct responsibility is the concern of deans, department chairmen, faculty, librarians and others.

The chief academic officer almost always comes from the teaching ranks and will have served previously as a college dean or department chairman. He almost always holds a PhD degree and will have established a solid record in teaching and research.

Chief business officer

This officer, usually known as the vice president for business affairs, is responsible for all financial activities of the institution — payroll, faculty and staff benefits, insurance programmes, accounting, budget preparation, financial reporting and investment of institutional funds. He is also responsible for personnel and staff relations, legal services, the physical plant, services and supplies, and campus security or police. He is responsible for the planning and construction of new buildings and facilities, remodelling and renovation of existing facilities, representing the institution in the purchase of property, and so on. In some institutions he is responsible for the bookshop, food service and housing, although these are more commonly the responsibility of the chief student affairs officer. If the institution has staff unions the vice president for business affairs is usually responsible for contract negotiations and union relations.

The chief business officer is often assisted by a bursar, comptroller, internal auditor, business manager, chief accountant and legal counsel, plus several directors who head such services as personnel, purchasing, police and physical plant. In a large university the director of physical plant alone may be responsible for a budget of $15 million or more and several hundred employees in building maintenance and repair, heating and cooling plant, custodians, gardeners and grounds keepers.

It is unusual, although not unknown, for the vice president for business affairs to come from faculty ranks. Typically he holds a bachelor's degree and sometimes a master's degree in business administration and has achieved that position following experience in the university business office.

Chief student affairs officer

Usually known as vice president for student affairs or student services or dean of students in some small institutions, this officer is responsible for student housing, food service, health service, counselling, career

44

planning, recreation and entertainment, intramural sports, student government, clubs, student discipline, financial aid, fraternities and sororities, and, in many institutions, admission, registration and student records, bookshop and intercollegiate athletics.

With such a broad range of responsibilities the vice president for student affairs usually has a large staff to manage various programmes. Until the 1970s most institutions had a dean of men and a dean of women but as the women's movement progressed these titles disappeared, replaced by deans and associate deans of students; these individuals are responsible for student life and activities, discipline, fraternities and sororities, clubs and the like.

Food service, housing, health services, registration, bookshop, intercollegiate athletics or sports, financial aid and career planning and placement are headed by directors. Admission is headed by a director; in private colleges this position is often titled dean because of the significance of student recruitment and admission in those institutions. In a small institution one individual may serve as both registrar and director of admission.

A student life and/or student activities director is responsible for recreation, entertainment, intramural sports and related activities.

Before the 1960s the chief student affairs officer was often a former faculty member or coach, but owing to the growing complexity of the position and its responsibilities he is likely to be trained in counselling, psychology, student personnel administration or higher education administration and to have served first in subordinate positions in the student affairs office. This position requires a person who understands student development and can deal with student problems but who is also a competent manager of what in many colleges and universities is a multi-million dollar enterprise.

Other central administration officers

The president depends on a number of other officers to help manage the affairs of the institution. In large universities there is often an executive vice president or provost, the president's chief deputy, who is responsible for overseeing most of the day-to-day operations of the institution so that the president has more free time to spend on external matters, including, particularly in a private institution, securing financial gifts. The executive vice president often comes from an academic background of teaching and research but occasionally from outside the university.

Also in large universities, in addition to a vice president for business affairs, there is often a vice president for administration, especially when there is no executive vice president or provost, who handles many problems that come to the desk of the president that are not uniquely financial. The job description varies widely according to the incumbent president's perception of it.

The vice president or director of development is a key person on the president's staff, especially in private institutions, whose responsibility is to attract gifts to the institution. This person must possess superior human relations skills, be an effective speaker and understand tax law in order to help potential donors realize tax benefits in their gift. This officer is sometimes responsible additionally for the university relations office, including alumni affairs and public information.

In some large universities the functions are separate and a vice president for public affairs directs the public information office and assumes an expanded role in representing the institution to its constituencies. The staff may include one or more persons who work full-time with the state legislature, office of the governor and other state executive offices.

The director of public information, also called news and information or public relations, and his staff attempt to keep the institution's constituencies informed. They prepare press releases for newspapers, television and radio stations, prepare and present television and radio programmes, conduct campus tours, host legislators, news media and other visitors, and use other approaches to disseminate information. In most institutions that office is charged with translating research findings by its faculty into reports that the general public can under-stand.

The director of alumni affairs keeps contact with former students through newsletters, magazines and meetings, both in key towns and cities and on campus. This office is financed in part by an annual voluntary membership fee; in some states public institutions are not allowed to use tax funds to support this office and must depend entirely on membership fees and other sources for funds. Alumni are important to private institutions, particularly in recruiting outstanding students and in helping to secure private gifts. Alumni of state insti-tutions also serve the same functions, if to a lesser degree, but are particularly valuable in persuading legislators and the public in general to support the institution's needs.

The college or university's legal counsel is now a key person to the president and the board of trustees. Every college or university now has legal counsel. Large private universities have staff attorneys; small private institutions often retain a law firm to represent them in legal matters. Many state institutions are required to rely on attorneys in the state attorney-general's office (state prosecutor) for legal repre-sentation. In such cases, one or more attorneys are usually assigned to work with each state institution.

Finally the most ambiguous position in the university is assistant to the president, of which there may be more than one in a large university. The person who holds this position drafts letters and other documents for the president, prepares reports as required, responds to many who wish to speak to the president, may write speeches and papers for him, and spends a considerable amount of time in liaison between the president and other administrators, faculty, students, parents, public officials and other citizens. This person is often but not always a junior faculty member.

Academic deans

Each of the colleges and schools within a university is headed by a dean who is responsible for teaching, research and service in that college or school and for faculty and staff personnel, laboratories and other facilities, and for students' academic concerns. The dean, that is, dean of arts and sciences, dean of engineering, and so on, is responsible for reviewing and approving actions by academic departments relating to personnel, curriculum, degree requirements, research, public service and other matters within the responsibilities of the college or school. In schools without departments, for example, library science, social work, architecture, and so on, the dean also performs duties handled by department chairmen.

The dean or staff members monitor student progress, place them on probation, suspension or dismissal for inadequate academic performance, determine re-admission, transfer between fields of study, determine when each student has met all requirements for a degree and so certifies to appropriate institutional officials or bodies (committees or senate). In many institutions the awarding of a degree requires the majority vote of all faculty of the college or university, which is usually automatic following certification by the dean that all requirements have been met.

The dean presides over meetings of the college faculty, establishes study committees and appoints members and adjudicates disputes within the college. He reviews and sometimes amends annual budgets and major purchases proposed by department chairmen, reviews departmental recommendations concerning appointment, promotion and tenure of faculty and other departmental actions. The dean is also the next level of appeal for faculty and students whose problems are not solved at the departmental level.

Department chairmen

The central figure in the conduct of teaching and research is the department chairman who is always a faculty member of the department and holds or is eligible for tenure. It is his job to see that course students' needs are offered and staffed, that reports concerning the department are submitted, to offer leadership in developing or sustaining the department, and to handle the acquisition of supplies and services needed by the department for teaching and research. He presides at faculty meetings and assumes a leadership role in setting out future directions for the department and its programmes.

The authority of the chairman varies considerably among different types of institutions. In many prestigious institutions the chairman is elected by the faculty and serves a set term, three or five years, and the chairmanship rotates among faculty in the department. The chairman may have very limited authority, only that allowed by the members of the department; his role is essentially one of carrying out the wishes of the faculty. The chairman is usually a professor but in such a situation he may be an associate professor.

At the other end of the spectrum is the more authoritarian chairman who, with the approval of the institutional administration, makes many decisions unilaterally, subject only to review by higher authority, and consults faculty only on selected matters. In this type of institution the dean may consult with departmental faculty only superficially before appointing the chairman and, after appointment, the chairman may occupy the position for an indeterminate period. Chairmen who serve for many years accrue power and authority through knowledge of the institution and how to accomplish tasks.

Most colleges and universities fit neither of the foregoing descriptions, but fall somewhere between. The chairman is usually chosen only after all faculty have had an opportunity to express their opinions and rarely is a chairman chosen who does not enjoy the confidence of a majority of the department faculty. The chairman has considerable autonomy but can act on matters involving selection of new faculty, promotion, termination, tenure, and on courses, curricula and degree requirements, only after consulting with departmental faculty. The chairman can sometimes act contrary to faculty recommendations on such matters, provided he can persuade the college dean and perhaps the vice president for academic affairs, that the decision is valid; however actions by the chairman contrary to majority faculty opinion are infrequent and if they occur too often are likely to lead to a change of chairman.

The chairman's role is an ambiguous one. Is he faculty or administration? The question has not been answered decisively; however most students of higher education consider him primarily faculty.

Selecting administrators

The selection of a president in a major American university is likely to require twelve months or more. It begins with a search committee appointed by the board of trustees consisting of faculty, students, administrators, staff, alumni and perhaps local community leaders. Some of the members, for example, faculty and students, are likely to be elected by faculty and student groups and some, such as alumni, may be officers of the alumni association.

The committee first determines the qualities in a president which they are seeking, including consulting with a wide range of campus groups. While many of the qualities sought are common to all or most searches, committees frequently emphasize in their searches qualities which the outgoing president lacked. If the outgoing president was strong in academic matters but weak in public relations, the latter quality will be high on the search committee's list.

The committee then advertises the position in national publications, writes to presidents and other leaders requesting nominations and, as nominations arrive, contacts nominees and solicits their candidacy. Until a few years ago it was considered inappropriate to apply for a presidency without first being contacted by the search committee and that remains true in leading colleges and universities; but now it is not unusual in less prestigious institutions for the president selected to have nominated himself.

After résumés or curriculum vitae have been assembled and committee members have studied them, the list is winnowed to a small number and inquiries are made of references and other sources, usually by telephone. Then a final list, typically five, or as specified by the board of trustees, is selected for interview. The board may authorize the committee to manage the visits to the campus and interviews or, in some cases, the board or its executive committee may manage campus interviews.

Often the process is much more complex, involving visits by committee or board members to an institution to interview a candidate and others with whom he has worked, plus several visits by the leading candidate to the institution before accepting the position.

The entire board usually interviews the finalists and reaches a decision on to which candidate to offer the position. The chairman of the board is authorized to negotiate the appointment and its terms — salary, insurance and other fringe benefits, house, automobile, moving allowance and other considerations.

In most cases search committees and boards try to keep the names of candidates secret and if they fail to do so it is not unusual for nominees to withdraw their candidacies. While it is sometimes flattering to a candidate for the academic community nationally to know that he has been considered for a presidency, even if not appointed, if that happens too often future search committees in other institutions will be less likely to consider the individual favourably. The task of protecting the candidates is difficult in public institutions because most states have open meetings and open records and laws that guarantee the press access to such information.

One of the questions committees must consider is whether to look to individuals already in the institution as candidates or to seek a person from outside the institution. Often it is useful to look outside the institution even though a qualified person is available in the institution, for symbolic reasons, for example, a desire to have a person from a particular discipline, to signify a redirection of the institution's emphasis, to emphasize an increase in academic standards, to avoid the appearance of cronyism and others. Sometimes an outside person as president can bring about changes in an institution that an internal appointee cannot. Two-thirds of the presidents of universities and community colleges and three-quarters of those in four-year colleges come from outside the institution.

The appointment of a new president usually invigorates an institution, stimulates new hope and expectations among faculty, students, administrators and staff. There is usually a so-called honeymoon period during which the new president has considerable freedom to make decisions and changes, but as those changes and decisions provoke disagreement he encounters increasing difficulty in instituting them.

The process for selecting vice presidents, deans and directors and other academic and student affairs administrators follows that for selecting the president, except that it is less elaborate; the president normally appoints the search committees and makes or approves the final selection. In selecting and appointing administrators, other than those in academic and student affairs, not all institutions involve a search committee; instead an administrative officer may be appointed to conduct the search and screening process.

The search process became more elaborate during the 1960s, partly because students insisted on participating and partly because of affirmative action requirements of the federal government. Institutions must be able to show that they made every attempt to secure applications from women, blacks, Hispanics and other minorities and that full consideration was given them in the selection process.

Presidents of private colleges and universities and public and private two-year colleges are often given term contracts, usually three to five years. In most public senior colleges and universities presidents do not have a contract but serve at the pleasure of the board, which means they can be dismissed at any time.

When vice presidents for academic affairs, academic deans and other academic administrators, including presidents if they come from an academic background, are appointed, they are usually appointed to a tenured professorship in the department of their discipline even though they may not teach. When they leave administration, whether voluntarily or otherwise, they have the option of assuming their tenured professor position in the institution, if they wish, and many do so. When faculty are appointed to administrative positions within their institutions they retain their faculty rank and tenure to which they can return upon leaving administration.

Selection of department chairmen follows the same process as that of selecting senior officers, except that the search committee is usually appointed by the college dean and is composed largely of departmental faculty. If the department cannot afford an additional faculty member that would result from appointing an outside person, the dean may direct the faculty to nominate one or more members of the department. This is especially likely when the former chairman returns to full-time teaching in the department, when a reduction in student enrolments has occurred and/or when there has been a reduction in funds.

In some leading research universities, faculty who are dedicated to teaching and research are often unwilling to give up activities to assume the department chairmanship. It is not unusual for all the faculty who are qualified to be chairman to indicate disinterest and for the department faculty or dean to have to persuade one member to accept the position with the understanding that it will be for one term, often three years.

In many institutions chairmen are not paid any extra, except that their appointment may be for twelve months per year rather than the academic year only and their summer duties may require no teaching. Virtually all department chairmen continue to teach and direct graduate student research while serving as chairmen; some manage to continue their own research.

Terms of service vary widely and are generally longer in private institutions. During the turbulent 1960s, turnover of presidents and student affairs officers was more frequent but by 1980 the average terms were longer: president 9.4 years; chief academic officer 5.5 years; chief student affairs officer 5.9 years; chief business officer 6.2 years; dean of arts and sciences 5.2 years; and dean of engineering 8.7 years. Presidents of public institutions serve for shorter periods; in comprehensive state colleges and universities terms average six years.

Compensation of administrators

Salaries and benefits for college and university administrators vary greatly with major differences between public and private institutions and between types of institution. The average salary of presidents in public universities in 1983–4 was $70 700 and in independent (non-church related) universities $90 000. In public four-year colleges presidents' salaries averaged $59 800 and in independent colleges they averaged $63 300 (*CHE*, 30 May 1984). Average salaries in church-related institutions are usually lower, due in part to the fact that presidents of Catholic institutions are often clerics or clergymen. Salaries in some of the most prestigious universities were $150 000 per year.

All presidents participate in institutional retirement (pension) programmes; in addition, in many institutions, especially private universities, boards of trustees purchase retirement annuities and insurance policies for presidents to induce them to accept the position.

Most presidents of senior colleges and universities are provided a house, a practice more common in private than public institutions. Only a small percentage of public community college presidents are provided housing. When it is provided the institution usually covers maid service, care and maintenance and pays for utilities. Most presidents are provided with a car.

Private institutions generally waive tuition totally or in part for children of the institution's president but this is rare in public institutions.

Almost all institutions pay the cost of the president's membership in professional associations and many pay all or part of the president's expenses in belonging to country clubs, luncheon clubs and other local organizations that provide an opportunity for informal communication with local leaders.

Almost all institutions provide their presidents with funds for entertaining official guests and a minority of universities provide some assistance to the spouse for the entertaining she undertakes on behalf of the institution. She is normally not compensated but as the women's movement progressed during the 1970s a few presidents' wives were provided a stipend for their services to the institution: approximately 1 per cent of all institutions, 2 per cent of universities.

The average salary of chief academic officers in universities in 1983–4 was $58 500; however the range was considerable. In a few of the prestigious universities chief academic officers were paid almost $100 000 per year. In four-year colleges the chief academic officer was paid a median salary of $42 000 per year but again the range was considerable.

In universities and four-year colleges chief business officers were paid $54 080 and $40 000 respectively (median salaries). Median salaries of deans of colleges within universities (and deans of schools in four-year colleges) were as follows: arts and sciences $52 500 ($45 000); business administration $53 988 ($40 000); engineering $62 350 ($42 100); medicine $99 700 (none); and graduate studies $50 000 ($40 400).

In some institutions selected administrators are provided with additional fringe benefits because of the nature of their duties. Physical plant directors, who must be available quickly in case of emergencies in buildings, are sometimes provided housing on campus. Chief business officers and sports coaches are frequently provided cars for their official travel, and in universities with major sports programmes, the football coach is usually offered many of the same fringe benefits as the president, as an inducement to him to accept the position.

Except as noted above most administrators receive only the benefits provided to faculty and other institutional employees (see Chapter 5), with one exception. Administrators and staff are twelve-month employees and are allowed vacation, a minimum of two weeks per year but as much as one month per year, usually depending on years of service at the institution. Except in medicine, land-grant colleges of agriculture and other selected cases, faculty are employed on a nine-month basis and are not allocated vacation; instead they take the same vacations as students — from two to three weeks at Christmas, a week during the spring semester, plus other official holidays designated for all students and staff of the institution.

Support staff

Any organization depends on the support staff to keep it functioning and colleges and universities are no exception. Support staff includes all personnel except faculty and administrators — secretaries, stenographers, printers, librarians, accountants, computer programmers, custodians, electricians, carpenters, steam fitters, cooks, and dozens more. Most of them work for a college or university, in part, because they enjoy the work environment and interaction with students and faculty. Many staff members of universities prefer their jobs at less pay than they would receive if they worked for the government or in private enterprise.

In some public institutions support staff are required to be members of the civil service of the state government, which subjects them to its regulations and also its protection and services. In many public and private institutions support staff are unionized and salaries or wages and working conditions are negotiated through collective bargaining; in twenty states collective bargaining by state employees is illegal, yet in those states support staff usually have employee organizations to speak on their behalf and to provide their members with services.

In institutions covered by neither collective bargaining nor civil service, staff employees are generally provided protection similar to civil service, requiring reasons for dismissal after a period of probationary service, usually six months.

Compensation

In state institutions with civil service systems college and university staff have the same pay scale as other state employees, with salary increases typically based on years of service. Where no civil service exists state colleges and universities construct their own classification and compensation plans. In either case employees are provided pension plans to which the employee and the institution both contribute, plus life, accident, health and dental insurance, and others.

Private institutions provide a wider variety of personnel plans for staff, depending on the size and affluence of the institution, whether it is unionized, its location (rural vs. urban) and many other factors. Since they must compete with state institutions private colleges and universities provide essentially the same fringe benefits that public institutions provide. In fact with the exception of a few very poor private colleges, primarily church-related, private institutions often provide better fringe benefits than public institutions, not only to support staff but to faculty and administration as well.

Management

Many academics avoid the term management as it pertains to higher education; it implies a degree of control and direction which they feel inappropriate. Much decision making in American colleges and universities, especially the better ones, is based on collegiality which places priority on academic values rather than efficiency.

Management of organizations of all kinds and especially academic institutions depends considerably on the ability of administrators to persuade members of the organization to accept management decisions. Even in autocratically controlled organizations employees are able to stymie management decisions through inaction, delays, and other overt and non-overt behaviour. Faculty, because of a high degree of autonomy inherent in their work plus generally accepted principles of academic freedom and tenure, are able to ignore many management directions with which they disagree. Hence administrators who come to higher education from military service and the business world dedicated to tightening up management are often frustrated and eventually find it necessary to seek a degree of collegiality in order to secure faculty cooperation.

During the 1960s and 1970s several management systems developed in business and in the military services were introduced into management of colleges and universities. Known by their acronyms — MBO (management by objectives), PPBS (programme planning and budgeting system), and ZBB (zero based budgeting) — few academic administrators have adopted them, although the business affairs components of higher education have instituted some of them. These management systems function best in businesses that involve production of material goods and those that are marketing-oriented. They require goals that can be quantified and for which measurements can be taken frequently.

Some colleges and universities have attempted to set goals, such as the number of BA degree graduates in English per year, cost per PhD graduate in chemistry, and semester credit hour productivity per faculty member by discipline, but these have generally not been very successful. While the business office in the university sometimes finds such measures rational, faculty are more concerned with kinds and amount of learning that takes place. These are difficult to incorporate into an MBO plan. When faculty set an objective of increasing student learning so that half those enrolled earn a mark B in a given course, other faculty then become suspicious that the teachers of those courses may achieve the objective by manipulating the marking system, consciously or subconsciously, or by omitting material from instruction that does not appear in examinations, such as affective learnings which are usually more difficult to measure.

During the 1960s when higher education was expanding rapidly and there were shortages of places for new students, money was relatively plentiful. State legislatures pressed public colleges and universities to accept more students and worried less about management efficiencies. By the early 1970s lack of funds was a problem in all except a few of the most affluent colleges and universities and steps were taken to control spending. Some public institutions received significant decreases in state funds, were prevented by law from borrowing money or raising tuition and found it necessary to reduce expenditures quickly and sharply. After reducing all discretionary spending to the minimum, some had to make further cuts and were forced to lay off temporarily or dismiss permanently faculty, administrators and staff. This was usually accomplished amidst great trauma, often with those most affected complaining that if the board of trustees or administration had tried harder necessary savings could have been achieved without dismissing anyone or seriously reducing funds needed for teaching and research.

As we examine the demographic data, which show that the eighteen-year-old population will decline as the century closes, it is apparent that further reductions and indeed closures of institutions will occur, although it is unlikely that enrolments in higher education will decline proportionately, owing to increased college and university attendance by blacks, Hispanics, women and older people.

The introduction of formula funding for public colleges and universities, discussed below, introduced several effects into management in higher education that are not altogether favourable. For example, all formula funding systems involve enrolment, which means that institutions are rewarded by state legislatures for enrolling additional students, whether to do so is in the best interest of the institutions or the state or the students. It is also a stimulus to keeping students enrolled longer than academic judgment dictates. In an earlier period universities sought ways to help students complete degrees earlier but the funding system now penalizes institutions that take such action. While it is unusual for an administrator to urge reducing academic requirements, faculty realize that when students are dismissed for academic failure the institution suffers reduction in state funds, and therefore there is sometimes subtle pressure to retain students whose potential for completing a degree is poor.

In some states funding varies by field of study, based on actual costs of teaching in those fields; for example, funding for engineering and the natural sciences is much higher than for the humanities, which encourages colleges and universities to increase enrolments in the former rather than the humanities.

Institutional autonomy

When state colleges and universities accounted for only a small portion of state tax expenditures they were not of major concern to governors and legislatures. The enrolment explosion of the 1960s and 1970s, which required massive funds for buildings and other facilities and growing appropriations for salaries and benefits, resulted in a national average of 10.2 per cent of state tax income being spent on higher education. As a result legislators and governors seek more accountability from public colleges and universities, which involves large numbers of reports and accounting to various offices of state governments.

About the same time public and private institutions began to receive increased funds from the federal government — interest subsidies and

56

loans for construction of buildings, grants for development of libraries and laboratories, student financial aid, research and training grants and contracts, and many more — all of which involved more accountability and reporting to the federal government. The institution of federal equal employment regulations and affirmative action required preparation of affirmative action plans and extensive reports to federal agencies. Regulations, inspections and reports to the federal government generally affect private and public institutions equally.

By the 1970s the high degree of autonomy long enjoyed by American colleges and universities had declined. Federal laws required public and private institutions to construct special ramps, elevators and other facilities for handicapped students. Most institutions found it necessary to institute expensive programmes to comply with affirmative action requirements and additional employees were required to prepare hundreds of reports for various departments of the federal government documenting compliance with laws and regulations. Although admirable purposes, the consequences to colleges and universities were vast expense, intrusion into institutional procedures and reductions in the autonomy academic institutions had long enjoyed.

Universities in three states have constitutional autonomy, that is, their autonomy is cited in the state's constitutions and legislators cannot enact laws abrogating it. None the less those universities are subject to the same federal laws and regulations as other institutions, and to most of the same state intrustions. When college and university presidents are asked to identify the most serious problems their institutions face, they always include intrusions by the federal and state governments.

The courts

Before the 1960s few lawsuits were filed by college and university faculty, students or employees; it did not occur to them that the courts would respond. Lawsuits that were filed were often dismissed with an admonition to the litigant to seek redress within the institution.

During the 1960s the US Congress passed several laws intended to eliminate all forms of inequality of treatment — racial, ethnic, sex, age and national origin. Since then the courts have been more willing to accept lawsuits from higher education institutions not only involving discrimination but other matters as well. As a result students, faculty and others have turned to the courts, usually the federal courts, to seek redress on matters that were formerly settled within the institution or not pursued at all.

Most courts tend to sustain the colleges and universities when it can be shown that written rules and procedures exist and were followed, unless evidence of violation of laws can be demonstrated. As a consequence colleges and universities have been forced to put in writing many commonly understood traditions of higher education and to rewrite others in language that will withstand legal tests. College catalogues and bulletins are perused by attorneys for institutions to ensure that no promises are made in them that cannot be guaranteed. This developed as a consequence of a growing number of lawsuits including one by a graduate of a leading university who sued his Alma Mater for failing to make him a wise person as, he charged, the college catalogue had promised. He lost. One state university system with fourteen institutions had more than 300 lawsuits under way in the mid-1980s, many of which involved medical malpractice in the teaching hospitals of its four medical schools.

Most college and university administrators see the increase in litigation in two ways. On the one hand it is apparent that many people who previously failed to receive due process and fair treatment are now benefiting from the new attitude of the courts. On the other hand a large percentage of litigation is without merit — some of it harassment of institutions or administrators — and is dismissed or settled in the institution's favour, but only after the expenditure of vast sums of money and administrators' time that might be better spent helping the institution to be of greater service to all its students.

Source of finance

Approximately 2.5 per cent of the gross national product (expenditures for all goods and services) is spent on higher education including funds from all sources. This compares with 0.63 per cent in 1932 and 0.46 per cent in 1946.

The sources of those funds for both public and private institutions are summarized in Table 3.1. Included are income from student housing and food services but not such income as vending machines, sales in bookstores and student supply stores, farms and dairies connected with agriculture colleges, income from clinics and hospitals operated by medical schools, independent businesses owned by colleges and universities and income from other auxiliary enterprises. Further it includes only income to institutions, not student financial aid provided by federal and state governments which is channelled through colleges and universities to students.

Major differences between sources of income are found in tuition and fees, state appropriations, private gifts and endowment income. The income from local government appropriations (4.4 per cent) is accounted for by community colleges, most of which have local taxing authority.

58

Table 3.1

Sources of income in all public and private colleges and universities in the US, 1981–2*

	Public institutions	Private institutions
	(per cent)	
Tuition and fees	17.6	56.2
Appropriations (government):		
Federal	3.0	1.3
State	56.9	1.6
Local	4.4	-
Grants and contracts (government):		
Federal	11.6	16.9
State	1.9	1.1
Local	0.4	1.0
Private gifts, grants and contracts	3.5	13.8
Endowment income	0.7	8.1

* Not including sales and services of educational and auxiliary enterprises, hospitals, independent operations and certain others.

Source: National Center for Education Statistics, reported in the *Chronicle of Higher Education*, 4 April 1984.

Income from gifts, grants and contracts to public institutions consists largely of research grants and contracts conducted by universities for private industry, although in certain parts of the country, particularly the western and south-western parts of the US, private donors have made major gifts to public institutions. Most of these funds received by private institutions consisted of donations.

Since data in Table 3.1 are average figures, further insight may be gained by examining differences among types of institutions, that is, doctoral, comprehensive, baccalaureate and two-year colleges (specialized institutions have been merged for this purpose). For example, tuition and fees accounted for the following percentages of income in different types of private institution: doctoral 67.5 per cent; comprehensive 71.7 per cent; baccalaureate 67.5 per cent and two-year colleges 77.7 per cent. These percentages are higher than often reported because of the absence of income from auxiliary enterprises other than student housing and food service.

In public institutions tuition charges vary greatly between states but there is little variation among types of institution. Most American taxpayers agree that instruction should be free in elementary and secondary schools since attendance is mandatory but that students

59

who attend public colleges and universities should pay at least a portion of the cost of their education. This is based on the proposition that students will take their studies more seriously if they are required to pay a portion of the cost, however small. As a consequence all public institutions charge tuition; in a few cases the charge is called a general fee but is tantamount to tuition. In addition to tuition charges all institutions levy fees for a variety of services and purposes, some of which are mandatory and others optional (see Chapter 7).

The federal role in finance

The Constitution of the United States does not mention education but the tenth amendment states that all matters not cited in the constitution are reserved for the states. The US Supreme Court has ruled that this means education is the responsibility of the states not the federal government. While there was an education bureau or office, as a sub-cabinet office, in the federal government for more than a hundred years, it was not until 1978 that the US Department of Education, a cabinet post, was established.

Except for the fifteen special federal institutions funded by the federal government, general financial support for operating purposes is not provided by the national government. Yet for two centuries the national government has from time to time made grants and provided subsidies to colleges and universities, both public and private, to help accomplish national goals. Most of that has occurred since the Second World War.

The first grant was the Northwest Ordinance of 1787 granting land to a development company to establish a college in Ohio. Several supporting grants were made after that but the next major grant was the Land-Grant Act of 1862, which was followed by legislation in 1887 and 1914, expanding that act.

Legislation in 1917 provided for federal financial assistance to state governments to increase secondary school training in vocational education, specifically agriculture, homemaking and industrial education, with small amounts of funds to colleges and universities to train teachers of these subjects. One of the depression era programmes in the 1930s was the National Youth Administration (NYA) which provided funds to colleges and universities to create part-time jobs for poor students who could not otherwise attend college.

During both world wars the armed forces contracted with colleges and universities to provide specialized training of many kinds for servicemen. The largest investment in higher education occurred after the Second World War when servicemen returning to civilian life could attend college with all expenses paid by the federal government plus a cost of living allowance. Similar programmes were established for veterans of the Korean conflict (1950–2) and the Vietnam war (1963– 72).

In 1950, as a result of the expansion of college enrolment following the Second World War, the US Congress authorized the Housing and Home Finance Agency to make loans to both public and private colleges and universities to construct student housing.

In 1958 the Congress became concerned about the small numbers of students being trained in certain fields of study considered important to national defence and passed legislation providing loans and fellowships to induce students to enrol in those subjects.

When students of the baby boom began to arrive on campuses it became apparent that additional college facilities would be needed, so the Congress enacted legislation in 1963 providing grants and loans to both public and private institutions to construct classrooms, laboratories, libraries and other facilities.

In 1964 the Civil Rights Act was passed to ensure that blacks had total access to all public facilities and services and to attempt to bring about equality. The Congress believed that equality depended on education and since many blacks were financially unable to attend college, the following year the Congress passed the Higher Education Act of 1965 which provided funds for student grants and loans as well as assistance to institutions. Since that time there has been legislation almost annually increasing funds for financial aid to established programmes or creating new ones.

One of the acts of the 1960s was the creation of a federally funded work-study programme, similar to the NYA programme of the 1930s, in which the federal government pays 80 per cent of the cost when institutions employ needy students part-time. Provisions were also enacted whereby low income students could obtain loans from banks and other lending agencies and the federal government would pay part of the interest plus guarantee repayment to the lender. In addition programmes were created to provide grants to students whose family income was low and additional grants for those from homes where poverty existed.

In 1972 the Congress extended certain provisions of the 1965 Act and added new ones. It also confirmed a principle concerning federal aid intended to help students attend college. Colleges and universities had argued that the funds should be allocated to the institutions which would make awards to needy students; the Congress decided that grants to students would be made directly from the federal government to students, not as grants to institutions, although college financial aid offices would be used to transmit the funds from the federal government to students. Since that time there has been a sharp reduction in funds allocated to institutions and, concurrently, increases in funding for student aid.

In 1978 the Middle Income Student Assistance Act provided for low interest loans to students whose families were not well off but whose income was above the low-income level. In 1980 amendments extended several programmes and provided additional funds for others. By 1984 federal programmes of financial aid to students totalled $12 000.5 million. No differentiation is made in federal student financial aid between public and private institutions. Had the Congress decided to provide student financial aid to institutions instead of to students, some congressmen feared it would have raised a constitutional issue concerning its legality. Since the funds go directly to students the question of support to private church-related colleges is not involved. On the other hand the federal government has provided funds for private institutions including some affiliated with religious denominations, which were intended to support programmes designated by the Congress as being in the national interest; but such grants always specify that none of the funds may be used to instruct students in or to further a particular religion. Thus seminaries to train priests, rabbis and ministers are not eligible for federal grants.

Grants and contracts

Colleges and universities receive most of their funds for research from the federal government, as explained further in Chapter 8 and, as shown in Table 3.1, federal government research grants and contracts account for a significant portion of their income.

In addition to research the federal government contracts with colleges and universities or makes grants to them to provide many other services. From time to time it funds training programmes of various kinds. For example, the National Science Foundation, an independent agency of the federal government engaged primarily in the allocation of federal funds for research, was allotted funds during the 1960s and 1970s to enhance training in engineering, science and mathematics. Part of those funds were devoted to providing summer institutes or programmes at universities for secondary school teachers of science and mathematics.

State funds

State legislatures provide about 57 per cent of the revenues received by public institutions, on average. Doctoral institutions realize a slightly lower percentage because of higher income from other sources, principally research grants and contracts, gifts and endowment income. Comprehensive state colleges receive about two-thirds of their income from state legislative appropriations, a higher percentage due to less income from research grants and contracts, gifts and endowment income.

Public community colleges receive 53.3 per cent of their income, on average, from state legislatures which together with 18.8 per cent from local taxing authorities totals 72.1 per cent from local and state tax funds combined.

Before the 1960s funds legislatures appropriated to public colleges and universities were determined on a negotiated basis. Colleges and universities prepared appropriation requests based on need and reasonable expectation of legislative support, their presidents appeared before legislative committees and explained the bases for the requests and the committees determined the amount to be provided based on funds available and their assessment of institutional need. As institutions grew larger and more complex, legislators found it increasingly difficult to allocate funds equitably among institutions. In addition this approach placed the institution whose president was endowed with especially persuasive powers at an advantage.

Most states now rely on formulas as a basis for legislative appropriations, however, the formulas used differ from state to state. The simplest formula provides a given amount of money to an institution for each student enrolled. In some states funds for community colleges are computed by multiplying the number of classroom hours each instructor teaches by the number of students enrolled by a dollar figure.

Most formulas are more complex. Some states have computed the cost of each element or function such as administration, teachers' salaries, libraries, research, maintenance of buildings, custodial services, police service, and others, and, using different formulas for each, determine appropriations based on the number of students enrolled or number of credit hours produced.

Funds for faculty salaries are computed in some states by determining the cost per student in each field of study; thus the amount of money a public institution receives from its legislature for a student enrolled in a science course would differ from the amount for engineering, education, business administration, and so on. Further, costs have been computed for lower division, upper division and graduate level instruction in all fields of study. Calculations are usually based on enrolments in each field of study at each level during the preceding year.

Almost all public institutions rely on special legislative appropriations for capital improvements — buildings, laboratories, sports facilities and the like. Many public institutions assess students to pay for union buildings and other facilities not used directly for educational purposes and a few institutions levy a fee to pay part of the cost of constructing classroom and other educational buildings.

Private institutions

Most Americans, if asked, would probably say that private colleges and universities do not receive any state financial support. For most of the twentieth century this was true and is still a fervently held principle among some private college leaders, but those institutions do in fact receive some state support in most states. At the last count all but eleven states provided some kind of aid to private institutions, in addition to student financial aid, which all states provide. But most aid is for specified purposes; few private colleges and universities receive undesignated general operating funds.

Following the Second World War private institutions with and without religious affiliations enrolled large numbers of students who were receiving financial aid under the GI Bill. As other student financial aid programmes were established by federal and state governments, these were also available to students studying at private and public institutions equally. As the Congress and state legislatures authorized special financial support for categorical purposes, for example, interest subsidies for classroom and library construction, private institutions were made eligible provided none of the funds was used to further a particular religion; in short, church supported institutions could benefit from such support if no sectarian religion courses were taught in those buildings.

By the mid-1970s four out of five states were providing aid of some kind to private institutions. About one-third provided direct grants of financial aid to in-state students attending private institutions and almost as many provided grants to economically disadvantaged students who attended private institutions. The state of New York provided subsidies to private colleges and universities in that state based on the number of graduates who were residents of New York State, as follows: associate (two-year) certificate $300; bachelor's degree $800; master's degree $600; and PhD degree or equivalent $3000. However, undesignated grants to private institutions by state governments is not a common pattern.

About one out of six states contracted with private institutions to offer programmes the states did not wish to establish or increase. Again, New York State, the only state that does not have a land-grant university, contracts with Cornell University and Syracuse University, both private, to offer land-grant programmes, and with Alfred University to provide a programme in ceramic engineering. Other states have similar arrangements with private institutions involving different fields of study.

About two out of five states provide subsidies to private medical and/or dental schools to train state residents. In 1984—5 the state of Texas provided Baylor University, a private institution, with $30 million for medical education and $16 million for dental education. The reason, as in most states, was that it cost less to provide subsidies to enable Baylor to increase the enrolment of Texas residents in medicine and dentistry than to establish new state medical and dental schools; when the supply of medical and dental graduates was ample, state subsidies to Baylor could cease. Other states provide similar subsidies for nursing and other health science fields.

Finally several states provide various kinds of guarantee when private institutions sell tax-exempt bonds which reduces the rate of interest the institutions must pay.

While private higher education benefits substantially from categorical aid from state and, in a few cases, local governments, small, non-selective liberal arts colleges, which are most in need, rarely qualify for special programmes of financial support other than student financial aid.

State governments established many educational institutions and social programmes during the 1960s and 1970s that heavily tax their ability to support. As a consequence there is little likelihood that states will be able to increase aid to private institutions substantially, at least for the remainder of this century.

Private gifts and endowments

Philanthropy is an important source of income for private colleges and universities in the US, as shown in Table 3.1. Americans donate thousands of millions of dollars annually to churches, educational institutions, museums and other non-profit enterprises. Generally there is a positive attitude in the country towards giving and colleges and universities have been very effective in persuading donors to make gifts. According to the Council on Financial Aid to Education donations to American colleges and universities in 1984—5 totalled $6000.3 million, of which 18.6 per cent came from foundations, 23.2 per cent from alumni, 22.5 per cent from other individuals, 24.9 per cent from business corporations, 3.3 per cent from religious organizations and 7.5 per cent from a variety of other sources (*CHE*, 7 May 1986).

Philanthropy is encouraged as a matter of national policy through federal income tax laws. In the 1970s the maximum federal personal income tax rate was 70 per cent which meant that a wealthy donor who donated $1000 to a college or university or other tax exempt organization reduced his taxable income by $1000 and his taxes by $700.

In addition most states levy a tax on all personal income or on certain types of income, such as interest, dividends or capital gains. The top rate is generally between 6 and 10 per cent but higher in a few states; however all allow deduction from taxable income of gifts to colleges and universities and other philanthropies, providing further incentive for individuals to make such donations.

In 1982 the maximum rate on federal personal income taxes was lowered to 50 per cent, reducing the incentive for philanthropy, yet the amount of money donated by individuals to higher education declined only slightly and temporarily. The 1986 tax revision lowered the maximum tax to 33 per cent and while the full impact of that reduction will not be known for several years, many feel that the long range effect will be negligible.

Many gifts are in the form of cash but some are in property, such as shares in corporations, real estate, livestock, works of art and other valuables, partly because of tax considerations. For example, if a man donates to a college or university property valued at $30 000, which years ago had cost him $10 000, he would be able to deduct the entire $30 000 from taxable income. If he is in the 33 per cent tax bracket he would realize a saving of $9900 on his federal taxes. On the other hand, if he sells the property for $30 000 the federal income tax on the $20 000 profit would be $6600; if he then donates the remaining $23 400 to a college or university, he would be able to deduct it from his taxable income and, again assuming he is in the 33 per cent tax bracket, would reduce his federal income taxes by $7722.

Thus, if the individual sold the property and donated cash, the net cost of his gift to the college would be $8878 ($10 000 cost of property plus $6600 taxes paid on appreciated value when sold minus tax saving of $7722 on the gift of cash). But if the individual donates the property, the net cost of his gift would be $100 ($10 000 cost of the property minus $9900 in tax savings), making the giving of the property that had appreciated in value decidedly to the donor's advantage.

If the donor lives in a state with a state income tax, there would be additional tax saving in each case but the saving would be greater if the property is donated rather than selling it and donating cash.

Some colleges and universities retain ownership of revenue-producing property, such as apartment buildings, office buildings, farms, oil wells and the like, but most sell the property and invest the cash in stocks, bonds and other liquid investments. Colleges and universities with large endowments employ a staff to manage the investments but many institutions with smaller endowments (525 in 1984) belong to the

Common Fund, a cooperative association that employs a staff to manage the investments on behalf of all members who share in the income proportional to their investment in the fund. The return on investment of the Common Fund in the mid-1980s was about 10 per cent, which for an institution with $100 million in endowment meant income of $10 million.

In 1984, 205 colleges and universities reported endowments with market values of $1 million or more; the top 100 institutions, of which eighty-six were private, reported endowments worth more than $40 million each. Harvard had the largest endowment, $2000.5 million, with the University of Texas System (fourteen institutions) next with more than $2000.3 million, then Princeton with $1000.3 million, Yale with $1000.1 million and Stanford University with $944 million (*CHE*, 17 April 1985). It should be noted that this followed a sharp rise in the stock market which increased the value of some endowments by as much as 50 per cent over 1982 totals.

Most gifts to colleges and universities are designated for the endowment funds, not for current expenditures, although some income is so designated. Many corporations and foundations make small donations to several institutions and authorize the institutions to use the funds for current expenses.

Foundations

As already noted, almost one-fifth of the funds received as gifts by colleges and universities comes from foundations. Federal tax laws are designed to facilitate the establishment of philanthropic foundations; however many of these foundations were established before the introduction of the personal income tax in 1913.

Throughout the twentieth century, thousands of foundations, large and small, have been established. In 1902 John D. Rockefeller, founder of Standard Oil Company, donated $1 million to establish the General Education Board and in 1905 added $10 million, the income from which was immediately dedicated to improving higher education. A major programme of the General Education Board was the improvement of education for blacks in the South, including grants to black colleges and scholarships for black students, particularly faculty from black colleges seeking higher degrees.

In 1905 Andrew Carnegie gave $10 million to establish the Carnegie Foundation for the Advancement of Teaching, which over the years has financed a wide range of higher education studies. Among its first studies was an investigation of medical education by Abraham Flexner whose 1910 report was a scathing indictment of medical schools that led to the closing of half the existing establishments (Flexner, 1910). Two of its most important projects were the Carnegie Commission on

Higher Education (1963–74) and the Carnegie Council on Policy Studies in Higher Education (1973–80) which together commissioned studies on dozens of topics and has had a major impact on American higher education.

Perhaps the most significant contribution of the Carnegie Foundation (eventually $10 million) led to the establishment in 1918 of a pension programme for college teachers. Today that investment provides pension programmes for 3 500 colleges and universities, specialized schools, professional associations, research institutions and other non-profit educational and service organizations.

The largest foundation is the Ford Foundation established in 1936 by Henry Ford and his son Edsel with shares of stock in the Ford Motor Company. By the late 1940s when both had died the stock donated in their wills to the Ford Foundation was worth $2000 million (Curti and Nash, 1965).

More recent tax laws have made it possible for small donors to establish private foundations to which they may make donations, investing the principal and distributing the annual income to colleges and universities and other philanthropic organizations.

Individuals who make substantial financial gifts to colleges and universities usually ask that the funds be placed in an endowment, with the income to support a given position, programme or activity, for example, a professorship or chair, a scholarship, library fund and the general institutional endowment fund, or that it be used for a capital expenditure such as construction of a building or establishment of a special library collection. Foundations on the other hand often allocate their gifts to current operating expenditures such as scholarships and fellowships, for special studies, underwriting conferences on selected problems, minority student recruitment, and other special one-off undertakings. Although foundations contribute to endowment funds and establish endowed professorships and chairs, some foundations have a policy of not contributing to endowments but only to current projects. Foundations are major sources of funds for research but they also support a wide range of activities in institutions for which funds are not readily available from other funding sources, such as a study of an institution's faculty talents, establishing a programme of faculty development, demonstration and testing of a new approach to teaching a single course or subject, funds for planning a new degree programme, curriculum planning, underwriting publication of conference papers, and many more.

Table 3.2

Expenditures by function of public and private
institutions of higher education in US, 1981—2*

	Public institutions	Private institutions
	(per cent)	
Instruction	44.0	37.4
Research	10.8	10.9
Public service	4.9	2.2
Libraries	3.5	3.6
Other academic support	5.4	4.1
Student services	5.6	6.2
Institutional support	10.6	14.2
Plant operations and maintenance	11.1	10.6
Scholarships and fellowships	2.9	9.0
Mandatory transfers	1.2	1.8

*Except for student services, does not include expenditures for hospitals, farms, independent
operations and other auxiliary enterprises.

Source: National Center for Education Statistics, reported in the *Chronicle of Higher Education*, 4 April 1984.

Expenditures

The distribution of expenditures, shown in Table 3.2, varies less
between public and private institutions than among types of institution.
With one exception most of the variation is due to size of institution.
Since private institutions are much smaller, on average, than public
institutions, and many costs of operating an institution cannot be
adjusted proportionately to enrolment, the relative cost of institutional
support is greater in the former. Institutional support includes general
university administration, costs of operating the business office, the
development office, news and information services and other costs not
directly related to teaching and research.

The major discretionary difference lies in scholarships provided from
university funds; this constitutes a major expenditure in private but not
public institutions. Both public and private institutions rely largely on
gifts and endowment income for scholarship funds and such funds are
more limited in public institutions. Federal and state financial aid
programmes usually provide adequate stipends for students to attend
tax-supported colleges and universities but not the more expensive

private insitutions. In an effort to recruit minority students, many private institutions whose tuition is relatively expensive award scholarships to these students to supplement governmental financial aid. Often this involves waiving tuition, entirely or in part.

Since private institutions spend larger percentages of their annual budgets on institutional support and scholarships, the percentage of funds spent on instruction is lower. At the same time the cost of instruction in absolute terms is much higher in private institutions, due primarily to smaller classes.

The differences in percentage of funds spent on various elements of cost in all public and private institutions (Table 3.2) is approximately the same in different types of institutions. For example, instruction accounts for 43.7 per cent of all costs in public and 35.7 per cent in private baccalaureate colleges. In both public and private universities expenditures for research exceed the average for all institutions, 18.3 per cent and 20.3 per cent respectively.

A major difference is found between expenditures in public and private two-year colleges, for example, 50.8 per cent for the former and 33.9 per cent for the latter spent on instruction and 14.3 per cent for the former and 24 per cent for the latter spent on institutional support. This difference is due in part to smaller enrolments in private two-year institutions but also to the fact that part of the two-year institutions are profit-making enterprises which require greater expenditures for staff and services associated with institutional promotion.

Although the acquisition of funds has always been a problem for most American colleges and universities, historically the management and disbursement of funds was a fairly simple matter. Small institutions with a small number of administrators, most of whom were also teachers, were not faced with modern bureaucratic problems.

The tremendous growth of most colleges and universities, the coming of federal and state laws relating to equal opportunity for all and increased requirements for accountability to federal and state agencies, particularly those providing funds for the institution, have led to a high degree of bureaucratization and financial control not heretofore known in academe. If the corporate model of organization had not already existed in American colleges and universities, developments since the Second World War would probably have required institutions to adopt it in order to cope with the management tasks they now face.

4 Degrees and curricula

For two centuries after the founding of Harvard College, college education was largely the privilege of the well-to-do, for whom such education was not intended to be of much practical value.

The democratization of higher education, which began in the second third of the last century and gained momentum with the passage of the Land-Grant College Act in 1862, changed the role of colleges and universities. National leaders believed that college education should prepare young people for useful employment and colleges should be available to the sons and daughters of farmers and mechanics as well as the wealthy.

In its early years college education did not carry the social implications it was later to reflect; most of the students were from the privileged class and college simply documented that fact. As the masses began to seek higher education, college came to be a route to upward social mobility and economic advancement. Degrees became evidence of achievement, for moving up socially and economically, and were therefore increasingly sought by young people desiring to improve their lot.

Parents who wanted a better life for their children saved for years in order that their sons and daughters could attend a good college, or indeed any college at all. As late as the 1930s families of the lower socio-economic strata would often deprive themselves of necessities in order that a child could attend a two-year normal school to prepare to become a school teacher. The brightest child might earn a scholarship to a state college or university where, with night and weekend work as a janitor or porter or other menial job, he managed to support himself through four years of study. This pattern accounted for a large portion of college students during the 1920s and 1930s when parents were able to provide little or no financial assistance and student financial aid was rare and meagre.

Degrees became credentials and were necessary for employment. Most employers came to view a college degree as desirable, if not essential, for persons filling many jobs, some of which could undoubtedly have been performed by persons without college degrees. Many employers decided that the additional salary, often small, required to hire a college graduate was fully justified by the superior knowledge and sophistication the employee brought to the job.

Degrees

The Bachelor of Arts (BA) degree was the first to be awarded in America and continues to be the basic first degree awarded in most of the liberal arts. As the sciences began to emerge in American colleges the Bachelor of Science (BS) degree became common. In the mid-1970s the Bachelor of Science degree was awarded by 82 per cent of the colleges of arts and sciences, in addition to the Bachelor of Arts degree (Levine, 1978).

When first introduced the BS degree was adopted for the sciences in some institutions because some faculty in the humanities considered the sciences inferior academically and unworthy of the BA (sometimes called the AB) degree. This prejudice has long since disappeared. In some cases the BS was introduced as a way to avoid the foreign language requirement of the BA degree; however it was the degree of choice to many faculty and students in the sciences who felt it more appropriate for their curricula.

The BA degree is identified largely with liberal arts (that is, arts and sciences) curricula; however in recent years as new undergraduate professional programmes have been established the BA degree has been chosen in some cases as the degree to award. This decision is solely the responsibility of the institutional faculties, administrations and governing boards in private institutions, and in state institutions the responsibility of those groups plus state coordinating agencies; there are exceptions in the cases of some professional curricula in which an accrediting body exercises indirect influence on the label chosen for the degree.

Most undergraduate professional curricula — engineering, agriculture, nursing, social work, education and others — adopted the BS degree. Some institutions added the specialty to the degree, for example, BSEE (electrical engineering), BSEd (education), BSN (nursing) and BSAgr (agriculture). The BEng, BN, BEd and other professional undergraduate degrees that omit sciences in the degree title are rare, although they do occur. One exception is the BBA which is popular with students, faculty and employers and is awarded by a majority of institutions that offer business administration, many of which also offer the BS in the various specialties — finance, management, marketing, and so on.

All bachelor's degree curricula require four years of study, except architecture and pharmacy which require five years. A few attempts have been made to require five years of study for the bachelor's degree in engineering, education and other professional fields but most such attempts have failed; students turned elsewhere for four-year bacca-laureate degree programmes.

Community colleges award the Associate in Arts (AA) and Associate in Science (AS) degrees upon completion of two years of academic study, and the Associate in Applied Science (AAS) for the completion of two years of study in vocational-technical programmes. In addition, more than a hundred four-year colleges and universities offer two-year programmes and award one or more of the associate degrees above.

Professional degrees

The Doctor of Medicine (MD) degree is awarded for the practice of medicine. The Doctor of Osteopathy (DO) degree is awarded by medical schools that emphasize bone and muscle manipulation; holders of the DO degree are licensed for the general practice of medicine in all states, but they account for only about 4 per cent of the licensed physicians in the country.

Almost all physicians receive specialty training after receiving the MD or DO degree; however there are no degrees for such training. Instead there are national boards of physicians (non-governmental) that certify those who have completed appropriate training in the specialty.

The Doctor of Dental Surgery (DDS), which is awarded by forty schools of dentistry, and the Doctor of Dental Medicine (DMD), awarded by twenty schools, both prepare practitioners of dentistry. Post-doctoral study or apprenticeship is not required; holders of these degrees who pass state licensing exams may enter practice directly.

The Doctor of Optometry (OD) engages primarily in fitting glasses but cannot be licensed to administer medications or practise surgery. The Doctor of Medical Podiatry (DPM) is trained to treat foot problems, but there are only five such schools in the US and few practitioners.

The Doctor of Veterinary Medicine (DVM) degree is awarded to those trained to treat animals. No post-doctoral training is required for practice, only state licensing.

The Doctor of Chiropractic (DC) is trained to treat disease through bone and muscle manipulation to adjust nerve functions but cannot be licensed to administer medication or practise surgery. Most physicians do not accept the principles upon which chiropractic is based and do not admit chiropractors to the medical community; however chiropractors are licensed in all the states. All chiropractic training schools are independent, non-profit making institutions.

All law schools in the country award the JD (Juris Doctor or Doctor of Jurisprudence) degree. Before 1970 the first law degree awarded was LL.B (Bachelor of Laws). In earlier times no undergraduate study was required for admission to law schools, hence the LL.B was the logical first degree; but as law schools began to require undergraduate preparation and, later, undergraduate degrees, for admission, law schools changed the first degree to the JD.

Graduate degrees

The Master of Arts (MA) and Master of Science (MS) degrees are standard in the arts and sciences disciplines and are also offered in many professional fields. In addition we find dozens of professional degrees designating the discipline, such as MEd, MAgr, MEngr, MF (forestry), MSW (social work), MLS (librarianship), MBA (business administration), MArch, and more.

These professional degrees developed for a variety of reasons. In most cases the purpose was to prepare practitioners rather than research scholars, and concomitantly to delete requirements believed less essential for practitioners, such as a foreign language. While the MA and MS usually require a thesis, most professional degrees do not and curricula differ.

On the other hand professional degrees often require considerably more course work and may require an internship, a project such as an engineering design, or in the case of the MFA an original piece of music, a work of art or a dance.

The MA and MS typically require either twenty-four or thirty semester credits of course work and a thesis, which is usually accepted for six credits. Professional master's degrees require a minimum of thirty-six credits, frequently more; in some institutions the MBA degree requires as many as sixty-six semester credits.

Frequently both the MA or MS and a professional degree are offered. In education the MA with thesis and the MEd without are offered by many institutions, and in engineering the MS may be offered for those choosing more theoretical preparation and the MEngr for those preparing for engineering practice.

Some institutions have modified requirements for the MA and MS degrees. During the 1960s and 1970s, the explosion of graduate enrolments heavily taxed faculty time and diminished their opportunity to direct graduate student thesis research properly. Further, in some fields, for example, mathematics, the large number of graduate students diminished the pool of research problems appropriate for master's level research. Faculties offered students the option of an MA or MS with additional course work but without thesis or substituted one or two lesser studies for the thesis requirement.

The Master of Arts in Teaching (MAT) was developed more recently and is designed for students who received the bachelor's degree in liberal arts and wish to qualify as teachers with a fifth year of study.

In the field of dentistry the master's degree is awarded for one year of study beyond the DDS or DMD but in the remainder of the healing arts the postgraduate degree is taken in one of the basic sciences. Many holders of the MD degree, especially those who teach or do research in medical schools, take the PhD degree in anatomy, physiology or other basic sciences.

The Master of Laws (LL.M) is the first graduate degree in law and the JSD (Doctor of Scientific Jurisprudence or Doctor of the Science of Law) is the highest earned degree in law; however faculty of law are normally not required to hold either to be appointed.

Doctoral degrees

The Doctor of Philosophy (PhD) is the highest graduate degree awarded in the US. Unlike research doctorates in European universities, which are identified by the discipline, the PhD in the US is the most common research degree and applies to most disciplines. The first PhD was awarded by Yale University in 1861.

The American PhD degree was adopted from the doctorate in German universities where many Americans studied in the last century, receiving the doctorate in the Faculty of Philosophy from which the degree took its name. For many years the PhD degree was awarded in the arts and sciences only, but as graduate study developed in applied fields of study the PhD degree had become so well established as the doctoral research degree that it was adopted in most applied fields as well.

In recent years the Doctor of Science (DSc) degree, historically an honorary degree, has been offered in a small number of universities as an earned degree in the sciences, and due to the prestige of most of the institutions offering the DSc, it is considered equal to the PhD degree.

The first Doctor of Education (EdD) degree was awarded by Harvard University in 1923. During the next fifty years it spread throughout universities, and in the 1950s and 1960s more EdD than PhD degrees were awarded in education. At the time Harvard introduced the EdD the PhD degree was reserved for its Graduate School of Arts and Sciences; all Harvard's professional schools awarded a professional doctorate and this is still true.

The EdD degree was introduced at other universities for various reasons. One of the most common was to avoid the study of two foreign languages required for the PhD degree. Until well into the twentieth century the amount of research literature available in English was inadequate to support PhD level research; graduate faculties required PhD candidates to learn to read two foreign languages, usually German and French, so they could read the research literature in their disciplines. Since the EdD degree was intended for practitioners rather than research scholars, graduate professors of education felt that other studies would be more useful than the study of two foreign languages. Interestingly, by the early 1970s faculties in most other disciplines had arrived at the same conclusion and eliminated the foreign language requirement for the PhD degree. By 1980 the EdD degree was chosen by only a minority of students in education.

The EdD, as originally conceived, had other values: it usually called for a wider range of course work with broader knowledge of the field of education and subfields than the PhD; it often substituted field research projects related to education practice for the dissertation; and normally it did not require as much continuous resident study as the PhD, making it possible for school administrators to pursue the degree during summer sessions.

Some of the same reasons apply with respect to the establishment of doctorates in other professional fields such as the DEngr, DSW (social work), DFA (fine arts), DPA (public administration), DBA (business administration), and others. Most of those degrees, when established, did not require knowledge of two foreign languages as the PhD degree then did, required much broader study of their disciplines, and stressed applied rather than theoretical research. Some, for example, the DFA, emphasized creativity and other approaches to new discovery that departed from typical PhD research. The DBA, except for the foreign language requirement, was similar to the PhD in all its requirements and since the foreign language requirement has been eliminated from many PhD programmes the DBA has been replaced by the PhD in some institutions.

The DMA (musical arts) is unique; it is awarded in the fields of music composition and performance while the PhD degree is awarded in music theory, music history and music education. The DMA, due to demanding standards by music faculty, is considered equal to the PhD in excellence in most universities.

During the 1960s the student revolution blamed the PhD degree, with its emphasis on research, for poor teaching in American colleges and universities. Except in research universities, which employ a small share of PhD recipients, the large majority of doctoral degree holders in American higher education devote most of their time to teaching. In response, several universities introduced the Doctor of Arts (DA) degree, designed for those who desire to teach in undergraduate colleges. Course requirements in DA programmes generally exceed those of PhD programmes in the same discipline but the dissertation takes a different form, often dealing with the preparation of materials for teaching the subject. The PhD in history, for example, tends to be highly specialized, concentrating on a historical period or region and supported by narrow, in-depth research, while the DA programme prepares the student to teach a wide range of history courses at the undergraduate level.

The DA degree did not gain popular acceptance in the academic community, principally because of the mystique of the PhD degree but also because the DA is offered primarily in regional or second level universities and did not gain sufficient prestige to make it widely attractive. The degree is still offered but its spread appears to have slowed, perhaps halted.

Post-doctoral study

There is no American parallel to the German *Habilitation*, the British Doctor of Letters, the French *doctorat d'Etat* or the Soviet Doctor of Science. The closest is post-doctoral study which is found most commonly in the sciences and engineering. It is most prevalent in chemistry. Upon receipt of the doctorate, graduates compete for a limited number of post-doctoral positions in universities to work with professors on research, usually funded from outside the university. This apprenticeship appointment is usually for a two-year period, sometimes for one year only, and involves a salary considerably higher than the individual received as a graduate research assistant but less than he would have received had he taken a regular faculty position. The experience leads to no degree but is highly valued for the increased knowledge he acquires in his discipline and the improved qualifications as a scientist; in addition the young scientist benefits by gaining a mentor, usually an outstanding scientist, who can assist him in securing a position and research grants.

Honorary degrees

The awarding of honorary degrees is a long-established custom in the US, adopted from the UK by early colonials. The awards are usually presented at commencement ceremonies and are made for distinguished achievement and service, often to members of Congress, cabinet members, state governors and other political leaders. In recent years a substantial number of performers have been awarded honorary degrees.

Small private colleges award a larger number of honorary degrees than state institutions and usually to businessmen who have made significant financial donations to the college or have devoted much time to its fund-raising efforts, and to clergymen of denominations that support the college. Many ministers perform worthy service for colleges of their denominations in recruiting students and assisting with fund raising for the college among their wealthy parishioners, and the colleges, especially the more impecunious ones, award honorary doctorates to such clergymen in considerable numbers.

The most frequently awarded honorary doctorate is the Doctor of Humane Letters (LHD), followed by the Doctor of Laws (LL.D) and the Doctor of Divinity (DD). As a general rule institutions do not award earned degrees as honorary degrees and vice versa. There are exceptions however. The honorary Doctor of Science (DSc) is awarded frequently, always to scientists; however it is awarded as an earned degree in the sciences in a few universities. The Doctor of Engineering (DEngr) degree is awarded as an honorary degree, though less frequently than the DSc, and in recent years has been awarded as an earned degree for those who complete a practitioner-oriented programme rather than a research programme. The last known instance of awarding an honorary PhD was in 1937 by Gonzaga University in Spokane, Washington, to one of its alumni, Mr Bing Crosby, the singer (Eels & Haswell, 1960).

The LL.D is usually awarded to government officials. President Herbert Hoover held eighty-one honorary degrees; President Eisenhower held forty-nine (Eels & Haswell, 1960). The LHD is awarded to persons in various fields of endeavour such as human services, social programmes, philanthropy, non-remunerative public service, and sometimes writers, producers, directors, playwrights and actors.

The DFA degree has a long history as an honorary degree and is the more commonly awarded honorary doctorate in the entertainment field but in recent years it has appeared as an earned degree in drama, dance and the visual arts.

Other more commonly awarded honorary degrees include Doctor of Letters (DLitt), Doctor of Civil Law (DCL), and Doctor of Music (DMus), not to be confused with the Doctor of Musical Arts (DMA), an earned degree in music performance and composition. An honorary MA or MS is virtually unknown.

Some writers on the subject have suggested that honorary degrees in America substitute for titles, decorations and governmental awards found in other countries (Brubacher and Rudy, 1958). Some state colleges and universities have a policy of not awarding honorary degrees in defence against efforts of political leaders in their states who would seek such degrees for themselves, their political supporters or friends. Only by having a rule against awarding honorary degrees can the institution avoid offending a government official whose goodwill and support may be essential to its financial solvency.

When honorary degrees are awarded it is quite likely that the commencement speaker will be among the recipients. It is standard practice in some institutions to award an honorary degree to the commencement speaker, in some cases a substitute for a stipend or to compensate for a small stipend.

Bogus degrees

Bogus degrees are common in the US in spite of efforts by the federal and state governments to eliminate them. The number of persons and organizations selling bogus diplomas grew in the 1950s but dwindled in the 1960s. In the 1970s the business began to grow again, apparently gaining its impetus from the expansion of distance learning programmes.

Even Americans are often confused by the plethora of degrees that can be obtained by post, some legitimate and offered by respected colleges and universities. The latest development appears to have been inspired by the establishment of the Open University in the UK in the late 1960s. From the beginning, the Open University was viewed favourably by academic leaders in the US. Soon a number of external degree programmes appeared purporting to be based on the principles on which the Open University was founded, some offered by respected colleges and universities.

Such alternative approaches to learning also stimulated the creation of a number of 'universities' whose function is principally to administer examinations and award degrees. Almost all are private profit-making enterprises that offer no courses nor have laboratories or other research facilities. Instead students register by mail and conduct research for a dissertation without leaving home. When the research is finished the external degree university convenes a committee of professors, usually from established universities, to examine the student, after which he is awarded a doctorate appropriate to the field of his dissertation. Advocates of these institutions point out that the absence of course work and the requirement of only a dissertation is consistent with requirements for the research doctorate in several other countries. Such 'universities' usually have an office, a small administrative staff, publish a catalogue and offer minimal services. The 'university' may charge the student from $1000 to as much as $5000 for such a degree. It is a very profitable business. None of these external degree universities is accredited by regional accrediting agencies; however several in California are accredited by the State Department of Education in that state.

The establishment of distance learning programmes and external degree universities stimulated a revival of diploma mills which provide no education and make no pretence of examination. They advertise by mail in national magazines and newspapers and sell beautifully engraved diplomas, usually for a fee of $100 to $500, sometimes for as much as $1000. The diploma is of no value if an individual applies for a position in a leading college or university, where faculty and administration will reject the bogus degree; but it may be accepted for elementary or secondary school teaching or in a small impecunious college unable to attract enough holders of legitimate doctorates.

In addition to bogus institutions, the instance of individuals claiming to hold degrees from legitimate universities they did not attend or from which they did not graduate is becoming increasingly common. This practice becomes news when a 'physician' who claims to have an MD degree is found to be practising medicine without a proper licence, which occurs occasionally.

The listing of unearned degrees in a résumé is much more common among applicants for positions in business and industry where it is rare for an employer to check institutions listed to determine whether the degrees listed were indeed awarded to the applicant.

Periodically state and federal officials mount a campaign against diploma mill operators and put them in gaol, after which the business becomes moribund, but within a few years diploma mills emerge again because they are highly profitable, requiring little or no capital, limited skill and primarily the ability to stay ahead of the law.

The academic calendar

Most American colleges and universities operate on one of two academic calendars — the semester plan or the quarter plan. Both are of nine months duration. There are three variations of the semester plan. In the traditional plan, the first semester begins in mid-September and ends in mid-January, followed immediately by the second semester which ends in late May. The early semester plan begins in late August or early September and ends at Christmas, with the second semester beginning in early January and ending in mid-May. The 4-1-4 plan is similar to the early semester plan except that the month of January is a minimester, devoted to concentrated study of one or two courses; the second semester begins in early February and ends in early June. The quarter plan consists of three quarters of ten to eleven weeks each; the first begins in late September or early October and ends in mid-December; the second begins in early January and ends in mid-March, followed by the third quarter which ends in early June.

Both semester and quarter plans allow several days for final examinations, as few as two days in a small college to as much as a week in a large university. It is also not uncommon to allow a free day before exams each quarter or semester, a so-called 'study day'.

Before 1970 the traditional semester plan was found in 72 per cent of colleges and universities. Between 1969—70 and 1974—5, many institutions shifted calendars, most from the traditional semester plan to the early semester plan. A 1984 survey of 3102 institutions showed that 58 per cent were on the early semester plan, 4 per cent on the traditional semester plan, 8 per cent on the 4-1-4 plan, 24 per cent on the quarter plan, and the remaining 6 per cent on other plans.

The trimester plan — three terms of equal length over the twelve months period with the first term ending at Christmas — was tried by a considerable number of institutions during the 1960s and 1970s with a view to equalizing enrolment during the three trimesters but the summer trimester failed to attract as many students as the others. Among other plans there are a variety of innovations and experiments. Colorado College at Colorado Springs follows a block plan consisting of nine terms of three and a half weeks each beginning 1 September and ending 1 June. Each block is followed by a four and a half day free period. A block may be devoted solely to one course on a concentrated basis or the student may take several courses spread over two or more blocks (Levine, 1978).

Summer sessions

Summer study is a major part of American higher education. Several summer schedules are offered and are usually unrelated to whether the institution is on the semester or quarter plan. The most common summer calendar consists of two six-week terms; a student is usually permitted to take two courses during each six-week term. Other institutions offer summer sessions of eight, nine and twelve weeks duration; some offer several plans concurrently. Six and eight week terms are especially attractive to elementary and secondary school teachers who return to the campuses in the summer for further study. Many professors object to the short terms, especially six weeks and less; they find the time inadequate for proper coverage of the subject matter of the courses, especially graduate courses that require considerable reading.

Enrolment in summer sessions varies widely according to the type of institution, field of study, level of study, and so on. In 1976, 38 per cent of students surveyed said they had attended one or more summer terms towards their degrees (Levine, 1978). Summer school attendance is higher in public institutions and lower in selective private liberal arts colleges (22 per cent). In one state university system 30 per cent of the freshmen and sophomores, 52 per cent of the juniors and seniors and 72 per cent of the graduate students attended summer session in 1980 (Montgomery, 1982).

Summer study serves different purposes for different students. It allows them to shorten the years spent earning a degree, to take a lighter course load during the academic year, permits the addition of enrichment courses to the curriculum, and enables them to retake courses previously failed or in which they had performed poorly.

Courses and credits

The American usage of the term 'course' is sometimes confusing to persons in other countries, such as the UK where it is also used as 'curriculum' is used in the US. In the US the term 'course' is used to refer to a unit of instruction, usually covering a semester or quarter, treating a limited topic of learning. During a four-year programme of study at a college a student will normally complete forty to fifty courses. Examples of undergraduate courses are: introduction to zoology; English composition; organic chemistry; industrial sociology; psychology of learning.

The most common meeting schedule for a course taught on the semester system is one hour, three days per week (actually fifty minutes each meeting, since ten minutes is allowed for change of classes). The three-credit course accounts for the majority of courses offered; however there are others. In the sciences a course is likely to be offered for four credits because it meets three times per week for lecture, plus once a week for laboratory instruction and practice. The laboratory session will usually be of two or three hours duration, even though only one credit is awarded.

Institutions that follow the quarter plan offer a combination of five-credit and three-credit courses, primarily the latter. Five-credit courses usually meet daily while three-credit courses meet three times per week or, in a few cases, twice per week for one and a half hours each time. A three-credit course in the quarter system is equal to a two-credit semester course since the quarter is only two-thirds as long as the semester and the student has had approximately two-thirds as much class instruction as in a three-credit course in an institution on the semester basis.

The typical course load is fifteen credits per semester or quarter; however the more able students often take eighteen credits, and in a few cases up to twenty-one credits.

The American credit system grew out of the struggle for electives in the 1880s. Previously the curriculum was rigid with all courses required. As efforts to permit electives at Harvard and elsewhere began to succeed, there was need for a way to tally completion of degree requirements.

The course credit system simplifies setting tuition fees and other charges, determining eligibility for graduation, transfer among institutions, faculty workload computation and the full panoply of activities associated with counting in the academic endeavour. On the other hand it tends to give the student the illusion that the compilation of a stated number of credits constitutes an education. The student may be so intent on counting the number of credits he needs to complete a degree that he overlooks what should be the purpose for which he is attending the institution — an education.

Course credits are used not only for courses involving class meetings — lecture, laboratory, seminars, and so on — but for independent study, thesis and dissertation studies, practicals, and other learning activities that contribute to a degree.

CLEP

The College Level Examination Program was developed for individuals who learn the content of college courses through experience, self-education or other means. Though CLEP was originally intended for adults nearly half of those who take the tests are recent secondary school graduates. CLEP offers examinations in thirty-four courses plus five general areas — English composition, humanities, social sciences-history, natural sciences and mathematics. Each of the five general exams is equal to a two-semester course. More than 2000 colleges and universities accept passing scores on a CLEP examination as credit for the comparable course offered by the institution. It is not unusual for highly talented freshmen students in college to receive one semester of college credit through CLEP exams and is quite possible for a student to earn a full year of credit in this way.

Experience credit

Some colleges and universities award college credit for experience outside college, principally work experience. This is highly controversial and is offered in few leading colleges and universities. It is more common in less selective private colleges and in community colleges, particularly in vocational-technical programmes. Supporters argue that it simply documents learning acquired through non-college study; opponents say it is not education since there is no evidence that learning took place and there is no way to evaluate it accurately.

The curriculum

Most Europeans find the American undergraduate curriculum strange since they complete their general education at the secondary school level. In almost all undergraduate curricula in the US the student takes a designated portion, on the average 20 to 40 per cent, of the undergraduate curriculum in general education. The general education requirement in a college or university applies to all students regardless of their fields of specialization and includes studies in writing, literature, history, biological sciences, physical sciences, mathematics, social-behavioural sciences and fine arts, usually at the freshman and sophomore levels.

The portion of the curriculum composed of general education varies considerably. In research and other doctoral-granting universities, more than two-thirds of the arts and sciences colleges require 30 per cent or more of the curriculum in general education, while in their professional schools (engineering, agriculture, and so on) more than two-thirds require less than 30 per cent (Levine, 1978). General education requirements in private liberal arts colleges are similar to those in arts and sciences colleges in universities. In a few institutions, for example, independent theological schools, little or no general education is included in the curriculum.

Few faculty are under the illusion that brief exposure to one or two courses in each of several disciplines in the arts and sciences will provide the undergraduate with an adequate general education. Each course introduces the student to some disciplines that are new to him and expands his understanding of others, with the aim of his gaining some understanding and appreciation of the humanities, social sciences, natural sciences, mathematics and fine arts. In addition to the academic requirements, the general education component usually requires a physical activity course that meets one or two hours per week for the first two years.

The undergraduate curriculum consists of the general education component, the major, and either a minor or supporting courses. For the student completing a major in history, political science is a common minor. The minor is usually found only in the arts and sciences; in professional degree programmes the major is supported by related courses, for example, engineering is supported by courses in mathematics, physics and chemistry (see Figure 4.1).

Suggested Arrangement of Courses for Eight-Semester Program

FIRST YEAR

Fall Semester	Semester Hours
M E 201G, Engineering Graphical Communication	2
M E 202, Introduction to Mechanical Engineering	2
E 306, Rhetoric and Composition	3
M 808A, Calculus I	4
PHY 303K, Engineering Physics I	3
PHY 103M, Laboratory for Physics 303K	1
Total	15

Spring Semester	Semester Hours
E M 306S, Statics and Dynamics	3
CH 301, Principles of Chemistry I	3
M 808B, Calculus II	4
PHY 303L, Engineering Physics II	3
PHY 103N, Laboratory for Physics 303L	1
Approved social science elective	3
Total	17

SECOND YEAR

Fall Semester	Semester Hours
M E 311, Materials Engineering	3
M E 324, Kinematics and Dynamics of Mechanical Systems	3
E M 319S, Mechanics of Solids for Mechanical Engineers	3
E 316K, Masterworks of Literature	3
M 427K, Advanced Calculus for Applications I	4
Total	16

Spring Semester	Semester Hours
M E 319, Mechanical Engineering Computations	3
M E 326, Thermodynamics I	3
M E 335, Probability and Statistics for Engineers	3
E E 331K, Electric Circuits and Electronics	3
Approved natural science elective	3
Total	15

THIRD YEAR

Fall Semester	Semester Hours
M E 336, Materials Processing	3
M E 338, Machine Elements	3
M E 345, Fluid Mechanics	3
M E 145L, Fluid Mechanics Laboratory	1
E E 131L, Electronics Laboratory	1
E E 335M, Electric Machinery and Magnetic Devices	3
American government	3
Total	17

Spring Semester	Semester Hours
M E 328, Thermodynamics II	3
M E 339, Heat Transfer and Rate Processes	3
M E 340K, Mechanical Engineering Measurements and Instrumentation	3
M E 344, Dynamic Systems and Control	3
E 346K, Writing in Different Disciplines: Natural Sciences and Technology	3
Approved technical area elective	3
Total	18

FOURTH YEAR

Fall Semester	Semester Hours
M E 353, Engineering Economic Analysis	3
M E 366J, Mechanical Engineering Design Methodology	3
American government	3
American history	3
Approved technical area electives	6
Total	18

Spring Semester	Semester Hours
M E 366K, Mechanical Engineering Design Project	3
American history	3
Approved fine arts and humanities elective	3
Approved technical area electives	6
Total	15

Figure 4.1 Programme of study leading to the Bachelor of Science degree in mechanical engineering, University of Texas at Austin

With rare exceptions the minimum requirement for the bachelor's degree is 120 semester or 180 quarter credits. Many curricula require more.

The term 'liberal arts' can be confusing. It refers to the disciplines in the humanities, social and behavioural sciences, natural sciences, mathematics and fine arts that are usually found in a university college of arts and sciences or a liberal arts college. In some very large universities, colleges of arts and sciences have been divided administratively into a college of liberal arts, a college of natural sciences and a college of fine arts, and on those campuses reference to liberal arts does not always include natural sciences and fine arts.

In some private liberal arts colleges and university colleges of arts and sciences the BA degree curriculum may not require a major or specialization but may constitute an extension of the general education concept. In many institutions the student is given the option, but the large majority complete a major. The major in liberal arts may require as few as twenty-four semester credits for the BA degree; however thirty or more credits is more typical. Those taking the BS degree in one of the natural sciences are likely to complete more than forty and, not uncommonly, more than fifty semester credits.

In professional fields the percentage of credits required in the field of specialization is usually greater, averaging approximately 70 per cent in engineering and 40 per cent in business administration (Levine, 1978).

Community college curricula

All community colleges continue to offer academic transfer programmes that parallel senior college and university courses at the freshman and sophomore levels, although the percentage of students taking such courses has been declining in recent years. In the 1960s and 1970s community colleges sharply increased their enrolments and offerings in vocational-technical fields, for example, auto mechanics, sheet metal working, welding, typing, shorthand, computer programming, electronics, television repair, and dozens more. Owing to a shifting job market these programmes proved popular and ample employment opportunity awaited graduates of those two-year or shorter programmes.

By 1975 more than half the enrolment in community colleges was in vocational-technical programmes. Of those students enrolled in academic curricula only a minority transferred to senior colleges and universities; in several states the transfers totalled less than 10 per cent of community college enrolments. Many students in community colleges who enrol in academic transfer programmes do so for other reasons: some to take a course or two, such as accounting or writing, to help them in their present job; some take courses in art, music, poetry, and others for enjoyment; some enrol to determine whether they want to pursue a degree and decide they do not; some enrol as a useful way to occupy their time between jobs, while others enrol for a variety of reasons.

Undergraduate professional curricula

In the early and mid-1960s colleges of arts and sciences in many universities enrolled as many students, that is, majors, as all the undergraduate professional schools combined. Beginning in the early 1970s that position changed due to shifts in the job market. Graduates with a BA degree in one of the humanities or social sciences could no longer be assured of finding a suitable job upon graduation.

New students increasingly enrolled in business administration, engineering and other professional studies. Business administration experienced the most rapid and largest increase and this is likely to continue for many years. In 1970 there was a large surplus of engineers. By 1980 the situation had reversed — engineers were in short supply and enrolments in engineering colleges expanded rapidly.

Departments in colleges of arts and sciences continue to provide courses to satisfy general education requirements for the entire university, but the number of majors in most liberal arts disciplines has declined sharply. Most students are now job oriented when they enrol in a college or university.

While they want their students to benefit from general education, faculty in undergraduate professional schools face the task of preparing them for professional practice in four years. As a consequence they try to include in the undergraduate curriculum as much professional preparation as possible. Not only are the general education requirements usually less than those in arts and sciences colleges, but total credit requirements in undergraduate professional curricula are often greater. While a degree in liberal arts may require 120 or 124 semester credits, in the same university a bachelor's degree in engineering may require 130 or even 140 credits. While it is possible for students to complete such a programme in four academic years, it is more likely to include summer session attendance for one or two years.

The bachelor's degree in business administration requires only 120 or 123 credits in some universities but in a large portion of institutions 128 to 132 credits are required. Sometimes the BBA requires more credits since its curriculum includes study in all business fields — accounting, management, marketing, economics and finance — and may or may not include specialization in one of those fields. The BS in business may be offered in the same institution with majors in accounting, management, marketing and finance.

Postgraduate professional study

Until the early part of the twentieth century students entered medical school directly from secondary school, but this has not been true for several decades. While many medical schools in the US indicate in their admissions literature that they will accept students with less than a bachelor's degree, in practice almost all those admitted (92 per cent) hold a bachelor's degree. Medical schools do not specify the field in which applicants should have studied but most pre-medical students take a bachelor's degree in the biological sciences.

Since the number of applications exceeds the places in medical schools, the schools are able to accept only those who show the most potential for completing the programme. The curriculum leading to the MD degree requires four years of study. Until recently medical graduates spent one year following medical school in an internship in a hospital gaining experience in all or most of the specialties in medicine before entering a residency programme in a specialty. Now however most graduates go directly from medical school into a residency pro-gramme of training in a speciality, for example, orthopaedics, surgery, dermatology, ophthalmology, neurology, and the like, most of which require three years.

The first two years of medical school are devoted largely to study of the basic sciences — anatomy, biochemistry, pharmacology, physiology, and so on. The third and fourth years, on average, are divided about equally between classes in medical science and clinical experience. The clinical experience is under the tutelage of medical school faculty in a teaching hospital which is usually adjacent to the medical school; in some cases the medical school is located in the teaching hospital building. Such hospitals are sometimes owned by the medical school but more often by a city or county government; only a few are proprietary hospitals.

Medical education in the US is very expensive. The student-faculty ratio nationally averages two students per faculty member. However faculty who teach the basic sciences (PhDs) spend much of their time in research and training PhD students in research, that is, in the basic sciences. Medical faculty (MDs) spend much of their time seeing private patients. While it is difficult to determine the actual cost of medical education, in 1980 it was estimated to average more than $100 000 for four years of medical education of which the student paid more than half in some institutions and less than 10 per cent in some public medical schools.

Curricula in dentistry (DDS or DMD degree), osteopathy (DO), optometry (OD), podiatry (DPM), and veterinary medicine (DVM) all require four years of professional school preparation. The distribution of time, by year, among basic sciences, pre-clinical professional studies and clinical instruction, is similar, in varying degrees, to curricula for the Doctor of Medicine degree. While most of the schools of each field of study state in their literature they will accept students with two or three years undergraduate preparation, most of the students admitted hold a bachelor's degree — dentistry 89 per cent; osteopathy 95 per cent; optometry 70 per cent; podiatry 91 per cent; and veterinary medicine 66 per cent. In addition to 130 schools of (human) medicine, there are sixty schools of dentistry, fourteen schools of osteopathy, thirteen schools of optometry, five schools of podiatry, and twenty-two schools of veterinary medicine in the US (*Health Professions*, 1979).

The curriculum to prepare pharmacists requires five years of study, including two years of general education and three years of professional preparation. This programme leads to the BS degree and accounts for the large majority of pharmacy graduates. In recent years more than twenty-five pharmacy schools have established a Doctor of Pharmacy (PharmD) programme requiring six years of preparation, four of them in professional study. PharmD programmes are designed to prepare pharmacists to work closely with physicians in hospitals in administering medicines to patients and in monitoring patient response.

The study of law has also become institutionalized. Until recently candidates could prepare for the state bar examination by reading law in an attorney's office. Now almost all candidates for licensing are graduates of law schools. All law schools require a bachelor's degree for admission, except for a few private schools which offer evening programmes. The law curriculum requires three years of study but no apprenticeship, and while the law graduate is permitted to enter independent practice upon becoming licensed to practise law, few do so but instead join established law firms.

Graduate education

Graduate study, both at the master's and doctoral levels, is intended to prepare students for professional work. In recent years a few universities have instituted a Master of Liberal Arts programme which is designed as further liberal education but this is an exception to the general purpose of graduate education.

At the master's level the programme is primarily course oriented, an extension of undergraduate study, although students are expected to spend more time in the library or laboratory and in independent study. Until a few years ago the master's degree always required a thesis and many still do, but in most professional fields, for example, education, business administration and social work, additional course work, seminars or special projects are substituted for the thesis requirement. The MBA programme usually requires course work only.

The movement away from requiring a master's thesis came about partly because of large numbers of graduate students, too many for faculties to supervise adequately in thesis research, but primarily because faculties and employers agreed that in some fields of study the experience of research and preparing a master's thesis provided less appropriate preparation than other activities. Master's degree students in education sometimes conduct studies of schools in which they teach, which may not be of sufficient import to justify a master's thesis. Students in social work are often required to complete an internship as a requirement for the degree. In some fields, for example, business administration and social work, the master's curriculum may be as specific as undergraduate curricula, and in most master's degree programmes there are recommended courses if not complete curricula.

The master's degree can normally be earned in one year by students holding a bachelor's degree in the field of study, but for a variety of reasons many fail to complete in one year. In some cases, for example, the MBA, the programme is designed to require two years. Students pursuing a master's degree in a field of study in which they have not had undergraduate preparation must usually spend two years completing the programme.

The term curriculum is largely confined to undergraduate study; when referring to graduate study the term programme is normally used.

Doctoral study

The American doctorate was modelled on the German doctorate and continues to bear considerable resemblance to German graduate education, especially in the sciences. In the basic sciences and the applied sciences as well, much of a graduate student's education consists of research under the direction of a professor in an apprenticeship relationship.

In other fields, especially in the humanities, the social sciences and many applied fields upon which they are based, a student is likely to receive more formal preparation in courses and seminars and have a less intimate research experience with his mentor or adviser. Except in psychology the student is likely to conduct research independently, consulting with his mentor only occasionally.

At the doctoral level heavy emphasis is placed on acquaintanceship with the research literature in the speciality. The programme of study for the PhD is rarely as specific as that for the master's degree. The student's programme − courses, seminars, colloquia, research, internship if one is required, and other experiences − is usually developed by the student and his mentor or adviser or with a committee of professors, based on the student's previous study and experience and career plans and interests.

Programmes of study leading to professional doctoral degrees such as DMA, EdD, DBA, DEngr, DSW and others are more likely to have partially structured curricula and usually involve more course work than the PhD degree but may require less time in research, on the assumption that people in these programmes are preparing for professional practice rather than research. This is not universally true however; in some institutions the DBA degree is research oriented. And in some institutions the PhD is awarded only in the basic arts and sciences disciplines, with professional doctoral degrees awarded in other fields.

Distinctions drawn above between PhD and professional doctoral programmes are by no means consistent in all institutions. Many institutions treat the PhD as a practice degree in some disciplines and require preparation accordingly. Hence a PhD programme in educational administration is likely to require an internship before receiving the degree, in addition to a dissertation. The PhD programmes in business administration in some institutions differ little from DBA programmes in other institutions, and occasionally both degrees are offered in the same institution with few differences. This lack of uniformity is confusing to persons from countries that have centralized planning and programme approval and indeed is confusing to many Americans, but it is an outgrowth of the high degree of institutional autonomy that exists in US higher education.

While almost all states have centralized planning for public institutions, few state coordinating agencies have attempted to standardize graduate degree programmes and requirements. In some cases they are unable to do so because the leading state university has constitutional autonomy, that is, the state constitution when written, mostly in the last century, specified autonomy, which prevents an administrative agency from dictating curricula, faculty requirements and other institutional prerogatives.

Private institutions have fewer constraints still. Hence a private university that already holds a charter could establish a doctoral programme in any subject and except for possible condemnation by a regional accreditation agency (which visits every ten years) there would be nothing to prevent the institution from doing so. In the late 1940s and early 1950s Michigan State College, now University, initiated degree programmes in hotel administration, police administration and other applied fields which met with severe criticism among the academic community as being unscholarly. Today such programmes are common in dozens of colleges and universities.

Graduate programmes leading to the doctorate require a minimum of three years' postgraduate study including the master's degree, but few students complete the programme that quickly. Those who do so are more likely to be in the sciences. Typically the student teaches or serves as a research assistant part-time while completing degree requirements. As a result the average number of years' study beyond the bachelor's degree for the PhD and comparable degrees, including only time registered in the university, is as follows: all fields 6.2 years; history 7.9 years; English 7.5 years; education 6.6 years; psychology 6 years; life sciences 5.6 years; agricultural sciences 5.3 years and chemistry 5.2 years (Anderson, 1981).

It is not unusual for a student to complete all requirements except dissertation, leave the university to take up a position and complete it *in absentia*.

In some fields of study, particularly in the more prestigious universities, students are discouraged from taking the master's degree if they plan to pursue the PhD degree. This occurs most commonly in the sciences and engineering. In some cases the master's degree is awarded to those who do not or cannot complete the PhD degree.

It is not unusual for a PhD programme in chemistry to require only thirty to forty semester credits of post-baccalaureate course work while a PhD programme in English or education might require almost twice that number. Yet this is not standard; requirements are left to the judgment of the student's committee, with only limited monitoring by the dean of graduate studies or graduate council of the university. While the number of credits for the PhD is usually less in the sciences, this is not always true. For example, the PhD programme in history at Yale University, which is heavily research oriented, sometimes requires only thirty-five to forty semester credits of course work.

Religion in the curriculum

In tax-supported institutions students are not required to take courses in religion; however many public institutions offer non-sectarian religion courses. Indeed it is possible to take a degree in religious studies in many public colleges and universities; such curricula tend to have a liberal arts orientation, and the institutions are careful to avoid the advocacy of sectarian views because of the constitutional requirement of separation of church and state in the US.

Many public colleges and universities offer no formal instruction in religion but allow religious centres sponsored by each denomination to be built either on campus or adjacent to it.

There are more than 125 private seminaries that prepare ministers, priests and rabbis, and almost a hundred Bible colleges that offer degrees in theology or Bible studies. In addition most private colleges and universities offer courses in religious studies and many offer degrees in religion, particularly those that are sponsored by churches and other religious bodies. A century ago, required weekly or daily attendance at worship services was common in private church-related colleges. Today it is much less common but is still found in Bible colleges, seminaries and some liberal arts colleges sponsored by denominations of more fundamentalist persuasion.

Military training

The first Battle of Bull Run during the Civil War was lost by the Union army. This sensitized the Congress to the need for a cadre of trained officers so the Land-Grant College Act of 1862 required that all land-grant colleges receiving federal funds offer military training. All eligible male students were encouraged to complete two years of military training but the last two years were optional. In fact the last two years were permitted by competition. Third-year students became cadet non-commissioned officers and fourth-year students became cadet officers. Upon graduation they were awarded commissions as reserve officers.

By the First World War army reserve officers who had been prepared in college through the Reserve Officers Training Corps (ROTC) provided three times more officers for the US army than West Point (Brubacher and Rudy, 1958). When the Second World War began the large supply of reserve army officers formed the core of the early regiments and without them the military effort would have been considerably delayed. The number of reserve officers serving in the armed forces was many times that of graduates of the service academies. Texas A & M University alone furnished more army officers than West Point.

Initially ROTC prepared only reserve officers for the US army, but in 1925 naval ROTC was authorized by the Congress and in 1947, when the air force became a separate branch of the services, air force ROTC was added.

Following the Second World War colleges and universities began to eliminate the requirement of two years' ROTC training, and by the early 1960s ROTC was voluntary on almost all campuses.

During the Vietnam war ROTC became unpopular and was terminated at some institutions, but by the 1980s it had returned on most campuses and enrolments were up sharply.

Before the Second World War, first and second year ROTC students received no pay and juniors and seniors received $7.50 per month. In the mid-1980s first and second year students still received no pay but juniors and seniors were paid $100 per month. In addition entering freshmen could apply for a competitive military scholarship and, if selected, received an award which paid tuition and other fees, books, and $100 per month for four years.

Academic honours

There is no parallel in the US to the BA (Hons) in universities in the UK. However most colleges and universities recognize graduates of high academic achievement at commencement ceremonies by designation of *summa cum laude* for the top group, *magna cum laude* for the next group and *cum laude* for the third group, although more institutions are recognizing only two top groups and are using the English terms 'With High Honours' and 'With Honours'. The criteria for honours vary. In some institutions designated grade averages are used; in others percentages are used, for example, 5 per cent 'With High Honours' and the next 5 per cent 'With Honours'.

Most colleges and universities have what is known as honours programmes for the most talented students in the arts and sciences. In honours programmes there are special courses and separate sections of standard courses that are more demanding. Students benefit by receiving an education of greater depth plus smaller classes and more personal attention from faculty.

In every college or university there are dozens of honours societies, most based on academic achievement and identified by Greek letters. The most prestigious is Phi Beta Kappa, a national honours society that recognizes high academic achievement of students in the arts and sciences. Tau Beta Pi serves the same role in engineering, Sigma Xi in the sciences, and for most fields of study there is a Greek letter honours society.

Licensing

In most professions a college or university degree is required for professional practice but in a number of fields state licensing is also required. All states require licensing to practise medicine, dentistry, pharmacy, nursing, chiropractic, podiatry, medical technology and other health professions. In each state the legislature has established boards of examiners authorized to examine and issue licences to practitioners and to revoke licences for malpractice. All of these boards are governmental agencies.

Law requires licensing by the state bar association which, in some states, is a quasi-governmental agency; in others the legislature has authorized the bar association to assume licensing authority.

Teachers in public elementary and secondary schools must be licensed but in most states teachers in private schools are not required to be licensed. Before the 1980s licensing of teachers did not involve an examination but instead required a college degree and training in specific subjects. In the mid-1980s several states added not only a written examination, in addition to existing educational requirements, but also required students planning to train for teaching to pass certain written examinations.

With few exceptions, for example, the state of California, community college teachers are not required to be licensed and then only in public colleges. Teachers in universities and four-year colleges are not required to be licensed.

Accountants are not required to be licensed but their credibility and ability to charge higher fees are improved by having successfully passed the Certified Public Accountant (CPA) exam, and indeed it would be difficult to make progress in an accounting firm without the CPA licence. CPAs and certain other professions require periodic further education in order to maintain their licence.

Engineers are not required to be licensed but many find it desirable, particularly those who enter private practice or consulting in civil, mechanical and electrical engineering.

Many states practise reciprocity, that is, if a person is licensed in one state he can qualify for a licence in another state by completing pro forma procedures. Often no examination of his knowledge of the field of work is required but in most cases, especially medicine, dentistry and other health fields, and law, he must pass an exam dealing with state laws relating to the profession.

While state licensing is required for the practise of many professions in the US, academic degrees have become prerequisite to certification and for many jobs that do not require licensing, although the degree is often an informal requirement. Employers usually assume a type and level of preparation for each degree programme, in spite of wide variation in the quality of programmes in different institutions, since it affords them an abbreviated and cost-free way to assess an applicant's probable competence.

A continuing debate in the academic community centres about the meaning of the baccalaureate degree. Once it meant completion of four years' study of a classical curriculum; later it meant four years' study of the liberal arts. Today it means four years' study. Except for the equivalent of one to one and a half years' study of general education subjects found in most baccalaureate degree programmes, the remainder is wholly dependent on the field of study and may differ among institutions for the same field of study. Curricula are determined by the faculty of each institution and may vary, although there is more standardization in undergraduate business administration programmes and studies in law, medicine, dentistry and other professional programmes, due to the influence of accrediting associations and licensing agencies.

5 Faculty

According to the US Department of Education there were 694 000 faculty in American colleges and universities in 1984–5, of whom 454 000 were full-time and 240 000 part-time (*CHE*, 4 September 1985). Part-time faculty included not only persons from outside the institution who usually teach only one course per semester or quarter but also academic administrators who continue to hold academic rank and appointments while serving in administrative posts. Typically these individuals return to full-time teaching and research following periods of service as administrators. The foregoing figures include only faculty of the rank of instructor and above and do not include more than 150 000 teaching assistants — largely graduate students — and other instructional personnel below those ranks, almost all of whom teach part-time.

The basic responsibilities of faculty are teaching, research and service. All faculty teach, except a small proportion in research institutes and other externally funded research activities who are often involved in training PhD students in research.

The extent of faculty activity in research varies. Research is a stated requirement of faculty in doctoral granting universities, and most faculty in leading universities continue to be productive researchers throughout their careers. In the leading doctoral universities it is now rare for a faculty member to acquire tenure without having been a productive researcher or having shown promise for becoming productive. However not all faculty remain productive in research throughout their careers.

During the 1960s when enrolments were increasing rapidly and there was a shortage of faculty[1] trained to the PhD level, institutions were reluctant to lose any teacher whose performance was acceptable. As a consequence most institutions retained and awarded tenure to some faculty who have produced little or no research since. The extent of this situation tends to be inversely correlated with the prestige of the institution.

In comprehensive universities, most of which grew enormously during the 1960s, the problem is magnified. Many of those institutions had been teacher's colleges and were converted to universities to help educate the baby boom of students. Their enrolments grew rapidly and state institutions were often unable to control enrolments; some grew from less than 2000 students to more than 10 000 in little more than a decade. The task of recruiting and retaining faculty in a scarce market did not permit the kind of rigorous evaluation before granting tenure that the institutions' administrators would have preferred, the kind that later became possible.

The extent of research activity in private colleges and universities is similar to that in public institutions. In leading private universities and selective colleges, beginning faculty must demonstrate research productivity to gain tenure. In less prestigious universities and non-selective colleges faculty are encouraged to be productive researchers, but in many institutions only a few faculty publish much of significance, due to heavier teaching loads, to the fact that these institutions are less competitive, and, in many cases, to the fact that faculty chose those institutions because of the absence of a compulsory research and publication policy, if not formal at least in practice.

Typically we find more research in universities with large graduate programmes and little in small private liberal arts colleges. There are exceptions. In a few private liberal arts colleges, usually the more selective and well-endowed ones, a substantial portion of the faculty conduct research.

Community colleges do not expect faculty to conduct research, nor do some specialized institutions such as Bible colleges, seminaries, art institutes, music conservatories, and some others.

Research productivity varies by discipline. In the natural sciences most faculty continue to engage in research, particularly in doctoral granting universities, due in part to the availability of funds for research from the federal government and other agencies. So do faculty in psychology and other behavioural sciences and to a lesser extent in other social sciences. Due to the availability of outside research funds most engineering faculty continue to engage in research throughout their careers. In other applied fields — business administration, education, social work, law, and others — the extent of research activity varies, generally in keeping with the prestige of the institution. In the more prestigious institutions faculty in the applied fields are generally active in research; in some that have only latterly begun doctoral programmes fewer faculty are productive researchers.

Service is more difficult to define. It covers a wide range of activities and varies in emphasis, both as to degree of responsibility and types of service activities in which faculty are expected to participate. Service activities usually include: service on committees in college or university department; participation in organizations and activities of the field of study at the state, regional or national level; serving on boards or committees concerned with research, philanthropy, social and humanitarian activities, and so on, outside the institution; and service on committees, study groups and boards of various governmental agencies − city, state, regional and national. It often includes making speeches to local clubs. In private institutions it may include student recruitment, fund raising and working with the religious denomination that supports the institution.

Land-grant universities with their tradition of public service, particularly to farmers and rural people, place high value on faculty members' service to the people of the state, as do some comprehensive state universities. Many urban universities do not expect the same level of service outside the university, although there are examples of such faculties being deeply involved in solving city problems.

In research and other doctoral universities outstanding researchers may forgo public service without incurring criticism from the university administration. Faculty whose talents and accomplishments in teaching and research are modest often make their greatest contribution in service to the institution or in public service.

Academic rank

The basic academic ranks in American colleges and universities are professor, associate professor, assistant professor and instructor, all eligible for tenure except instructor. Other titles, not eligible for tenure, include lecturer, teaching assistant, teaching fellow, research assistant and research associate, plus professorial titles preceded by visiting, adjunct or clinical. In 1981−2 the full-time instructional faculty in all American colleges and universities were distributed by rank as follows: professor 26.5 per cent; associate professor 24.5 per cent; assistant professor 24.4 per cent; instructor 7.8 per cent; lecturer 1.6 per cent; and no rank 15.2 per cent. However owing to a reduction of new faculty into academe the percentages of faculty in higher ranks continue to rise each year.

Professors, often called full professors to distinguish them from other ranks, are relied on heavily by the institution to ensure academic quality and standards. Committees of professors are expected to make initial determinations concerning retention or dismissal, tenure and promotion of faculty of lower rank; their recommendations are usually accepted by institutional administrators. In many institutions full professors make initial determinations regarding salaries and the budget for the department. The term 'professor' is also used in the generic sense to refer to all faculty; the two usages can often be differentiated only by the context of use.

Full professors also enjoy privileges such as choice of courses to teach and not to teach, student assistants, offices, laboratory space, equipment, working conditions, parking and others, although the differences in privileges between senior and junior faculty declined during the 1960s, a consequence of student and junior faculty activism and egalitarian pressures. The rank of professor in a European university, if it has only one per institute or department, cannot be equated with that in America where several full professors are usually found in a single department, and, indeed, in not a few colleges and universities all members of a department may be full professors due to lack of turnover.

Associate professors are considered by those who study faculty behaviour to be the most productive in research of all ranks. They usually hold tenure and are not distracted by the need to qualify for it, at the same time they are young and energetic and are working towards qualifying for full professorship.

The normal rank for beginning faculty who hold the doctorate or other appropriate terminal degree is assistant professor. In most colleges and universities the assistant professor is evaluated annually and if found deficient or inappropriate for the institution is terminated, usually with up to one year's notice. In other institutions assistant professors are initially appointed for three years, at the end of which they are reappointed for three years or terminated; at the end of six years they are either terminated or given tenure, that is, a permanent appointment.

The rank of instructor includes several different categories of teacher. In research universities it includes temporary faculty with master's degrees, most of whom teach freshman and sophomore courses only, some of whom are spouses of graduate students. It also includes newly appointed faculty who arrive without having completed the dissertation; when the dissertation is completed and the degree received they are promoted to assistant professor. It includes full-time faculty who are pursuing graduate study in the institution on a part-time basis, in contrast to other appointees who are part-time employees while pursuing graduate study.

In community colleges and many non-selective liberal arts colleges, permanent faculty are appointed with training of less than doctoral level; they usually begin at the instructor rank. Some community colleges do not have differentiated ranks; instead all teachers have the same title, usually instructor. The term instructor is commonly used in the generic sense to refer to all teachers in community colleges, and sometimes in senior colleges and universities as well.

Many doctoral granting universities have a policy limiting instructors to five or seven years' appointment after which they must qualify for promotion or be terminated.

Before the Second World War initial appointment of doctoral degree holders was commonly at the instructor rank but this disappeared during the 1960s when faculty were scarce. By the mid-1970s, due to availability of qualified faculty candidates, a few leading universities began to make some initial appointments again at the instructor rank.

There are several titles for graduate students who teach part-time while completing degrees. Assistant instructor and teaching fellow usually denote an advanced graduate student who holds a master's degree or equivalent. Teaching assistant is the most common term; in most doctoral universities it applies to graduate students who are part-time teachers regardless of experience, while in others it denotes those in their first or second year of graduate study.

Research assistant, usually the counterpart of teaching assistant, is appointed for research only. However research assistant and, more particularly, research associate titles apply to some full-time researchers, many of whom would qualify for tenured appointments, who work on research projects financed by outside grants or contracts.

In research institutes and other research programmes that have continuing funding for research, researchers are likely to hold appointments as professor, associate professor or assistant professor, or may hold those ranks preceded by the term 'research', and are eligible for tenure.

The rank of lecturer is the most flexible of all titles and most often applies to part-time teachers who teach one course occasionally but in some institutions also applies to faculty appointed full-time temporarily. The lecturer is not eligible for tenure and qualifications for the rank range from those required for a full professorship to those which would not qualify for a full-time appointment. For example, the University of Maryland, which has conducted undergraduate courses in more than thirty countries for the US military forces since the Second World War, appoints all teachers in that programme to the rank of lecturer regardless of degrees or other qualifications, whether full-time or part-time.

Individuals invited to an institution from another university to teach one or two years are titled visiting professor, visiting associate professor or visiting assistant professor.

The titles adjunct professor, adjunct associate professor and adjunct assistant professor refer to a part-time teacher whose qualifications are equal to those in tenured positions, who is employed full-time elsewhere and has a continuing relationship with the university. Often the individual is a researcher who supervises thesis research or provides research facilities and opportunities for graduate students and serves on examining committees. More often the adjunct faculty member is a person of notable scholarly or scientific accomplishments who teaches a course regularly, unlike some lecturers who teach only occasionally. Rarely, a tenured faculty member in one discipline will hold an adjunct appointment in another discipline in a university.

A clinical professor, clinical associate professor or clinical assistant professor is a faculty member in a medical school who usually teaches no theory courses but supervises medical students in their clinical training.

The most coveted faculty position in any college or university is an endowed chair. It is established by a gift of money or property which can be converted to money, from a donor whose name usually is attached to the chair, for example, the John T. Jones Chair in History; the holder is known as the John T. Jones Professor of History. The funds are invested and the income used to pay the salary and benefits of the chairholder and, in some cases, those of a secretary, assistants and research and other professional expenses. Most institutions require a minimum of $750 000 from a donor to establish an endowed chair, many require $1 million and some require $1.5 million; the least amount required by any university in the mid-1980s was $500 000.

A limited number of institutions have endowed professorships, in addition to chairs, which can be established with a gift of $100 000 to $200 000, which is invested and the income used to supplement the salary or support research expenses of a professor. The professorship is usually named for the donor. Both chairs and professorships may be filled only by full professors. In some institutions a gift of $50 000 can establish an endowed fellowship which is invested and the income used to supplement the salary of an associate professor, whose title may be, for example, Associate Professor and the John T. Jones Fellow in Geology. Appointment to a fellowship is normally on an annual basis. Appointments to chairs and professorships are usually permanent, but may be for five-year terms or, in some cases, annual.

Tenure

Almost all senior colleges and universities and most community colleges award tenure to faculty after a period of probationary service, usually seven years but of different duration in some institutions.

Upon the award of tenure the faculty member can be dismissed only for gross negligence of duties, gross incompetence, moral turpitude or conviction of a felonious crime or treason and must first be afforded due process, including a hearing before peers, examination of evidence and opportunity for refutation.

In many institutions, particularly leading universities, professors and associate professors acquire tenure upon promotion or appointment to those ranks. In others they must serve a probationary period, usually less than seven years.

Tenure has been severely criticized by political leaders, businessmen and others outside academe in recent years and by some within academe as well, on the basis that it provides a sinecure for faculty who are no longer effective teachers, who mistreat students, who abuse their position or in other ways are no longer worthy of appointment to the institution. Although all institutions have established procedures for dismissing tenured faculty, it occurs rarely. Incompetence and ineffectiveness are matters of opinion and are difficult to prove. The accused professor is normally accorded the benefit of any doubt that a hearing committe may have. The inability of institutions to dismiss faculty who are widely believed to be unworthy of continued appointment further reinforces criticism of tenure. While the legislatures of several states have considered abolishing tenure in public institutions, none has done so.

Several institutions established in the 1960s and 1970s instituted alternative plans to traditional tenure, including seven-year appointments, three-year rolling contracts and annual contracts. All these have been strongly opposed by the American Association of University Professors (AAUP), the long-term watcher of tenure and academic freedom in American colleges and universities.

Dismissal of tenured faculty in connection with financial retrenchment is the subject of much controversy. The AAUP position is that it is acceptable only if all other options have been exhausted and dismissal of tenured faculty is the only way to avoid closing the institution. Critics argue that this means that an institution would have to dismiss untenured faculty in a rapidly growing field, such as business administration, which might be understaffed, while retaining tenured faculty in a field where enrolment has declined and there were surplus faculty.

The courts do not agree with the AAUP on this issue. In several cases AAUP has censured insitutions for dismissing tenured faculty during retrenchment but when those faculty sued the institution, the courts have almost always ruled that the institutions were justified in dismissing tenured faculty where the process was fair and unbiased.

Many institutions are overtenured. Enrolments grew rapidly in the 1960s and early 1970s and in many institutions have remained flat or declined since then. As a result as many as 80 per cent and in a few cases 90 per cent of the teachers are tenured, which makes possible the introduction of little new blood into the faculty. Some institutions have instituted tenure quotas which require dismissal of untenured faculty after the probationary period or extension of probation until a tenured vacancy occurs. Others have sharply decreased the percentage of probationary faculty who earn tenure; in one prestigious university in the north-eastern part of the country only 15 per cent of assistant professors were earning tenure in the mid-1980s. On the other hand in some less prestigious liberal arts colleges 75 or 80 per cent of the assistant professors were retained and received tenure.

In a 1984 national survey of 5000 faculty members in all types of colleges and universities, except specialized institutions, the Carnegie Foundation for the Advancement of Teaching found that 35.7 per cent of the faculty polled said that higher education would be improved by abolishing tenure. About a quarter of the respondents were untenured, many with little hope of earning tenure; this undoubtedly influenced their responses (*CHE*, 18 December 1985).

Academic freedom

The main justification for tenure is to ensure academic freedom. While limits on academic freedom are now less evident in American higher education, there have been many cases in its history where such freedom was violated.

In earlier times when the general populace was less sophisticated concerning civil rights and did not understand the principles of academic freedom, it was subject to greater threat. As the educational level of the public grows, that threat diminishes. Even among educated people, however, there is an occasional outcry and call for dismissal of faculty who voice radical or unpopular views. The principle of academic freedom not only protects the faculty member but gives the institution's administration a basis for responding to politicians and others who demand the ousting of a faculty member whose public statements are unpopular.

Those who oppose tenure and the ills that accompany it argue that the major reason for it no longer applies, for several reasons. When the AAUP was established in 1915 the courts in the US did not often

104

accept cases involving academic freedom. Since the 1960s however faculty who feel they have been mistreated have been able to seek redress in the courts and have often succeeded. Secondly public demand for curtailment of academic freedom is now less threatening. Thirdly university administrators, most of whom come from the teaching ranks themselves, value academic freedom and are loath to violate it. Finally in most institutions an administrator who attempted to limit academic freedom would face a wrathful faculty who, if so disposed, could often engineer his dismissal.

Some critics of academe argue that the greatest threat to academic freedom is not from administrators or boards of trustees but from the tyranny of faculty and students. During the turbulent 1960s faculty who voiced unpopular views were occasionally shouted into silence by students and harassed for their views. And today, it is argued, junior faculty who espouse Keynesian economics have little chance of gaining tenure in some economics departments while in others only those who support that point of view are tenured. During the 1930s, 1940s and 1950s in some schools of education faculty who did not espouse the educational philosophies of John Dewey were judged by faculty committees as not worthy of appointment or tenure.

While totally unfettered academic freedom for all faculty, tenured and untenured, will probably never become a reality, when viewed within the context of the last seventy-five years we must conclude that academic freedom is in relatively good condition in American colleges and universities.

Qualifications for appointment

In all leading colleges and universities and most others, except community colleges, the doctorate is now required for appointment to a tenure track position. Some less selective private liberal arts colleges and specialized institutions desire but do not require the doctorate for new appointees.

In some disciplines the doctorate is not required. In the performing arts, especially drama and dance, the Master of Fine Arts (MFA) is considered the terminal degree. In architecture the master's degree is considered adequate, and in journalism experience is sometimes accepted in lieu of advanced degrees.

In addition persons of prominence or high achievement are sometimes appointed to academic posts although they lack academic credentials, including former governors, ambassadors, senators, senior officials of the federal government and other political leaders, performing artists, playwrights, authors, actors and other artists.

In fields of study where there are shortages of faculty, such as business administration, computer science and engineering, faculty without the doctorate are appointed, more often in less prestigious institutions.

Before the 1970s only the most prestigious institutions could require the doctorate for appointment; others found it necessary to appoint faculty without doctorates to teach rapidly expanding enrolments. As a consequence many institutions that now require the doctorate still have faculty appointed in the 1960s or early 1970s without the doctorate, and only have 60 or 65 per cent doctoral degree holders in their faculty. In many less selective liberal arts colleges less than 50 per cent of the faculty hold the doctorate.

Community colleges do not require the doctorate as a rule, however most community colleges have several faculty with doctoral degrees. The usual requirement for teaching academic courses in community colleges is the master's degree. Teachers of vocational-technical subjects in community colleges often hold no degree but are selected based on their work qualifications. They are often skilled technicians with many years of industrial experience and because of a shortage of such teachers to teach technical courses they are often paid more than teachers of academic subjects with advanced degrees.

Preparation for teaching

PhD degree programmes are research oriented. American graduate schools prepare students well for research careers but preparation for teaching varies, in spite of the fact that except in the sciences and engineering most PhD degree recipients become teachers.

The student rebellion of the 1960s was related in part to poor teaching in research universities, to inadequate attention to undergraduate student education and to what students viewed as overemphasis on research. Many faculty and administrators agreed and used the criticism as a basis for taking steps to improve teaching and the preparation of teachers. Since that time concern about teaching has grown considerably and criticism of teaching has diminished appreciably.

In many universities departments that prepare doctoral students now provide both training and experience in teaching. Many doctoral students are employed part-time as teaching assistants to pay for their education, but those who are not are often required, as part of their doctoral training, to teach one course under the guidance of a senior professor. In addition many departments require all doctoral students to enrol in a seminar on teaching conducted by that department.

For many years schools of education have offered courses in college teaching and some faculty in other fields of study encourage their doctoral students to enrol, but few doctoral students enrol in such courses, due primarily to prejudice towards pedagogy and schools of education. When such courses are offered in the department in which they are studying, this barrier disappears; both students and faculty have responded well to departmental seminars on teaching.

Specialization

Preparation for research requires intense specialization. As a consequence those who complete PhD programmes are usually well prepared in a narrow area or field of study but are often not qualified to teach broadly. The new faculty member may have received his PhD in history but is likely to have concentrated on a specific period or locale such as central European diplomatic history, history of the south-western US, Chinese history or early American history. If he takes up a post involving primarily undergraduate teaching he is probably able to teach only one course per year involving his specialization, out of some six to eight courses taught annually. This is not to suggest that he cannot teach courses outside his specialty competently, albeit with much independent study and preparation, but rather that high levels of specialization inhibit broader knowledge and interest in the discipline.

Reaction to excessive specialization led to the creation of the Doctor of Arts degree and, in part, to other doctoral degrees in academic disciplines, for example, the Doctor of Business Administration, Doctor of Social Work, and others. It also led some departments to make adjustments in PhD degree requirements. For example, several years ago the faculty of the Department of English at Johns Hopkins University decided to accept two smaller studies in lieu of the traditional dissertation which required three, four, five or more years to complete.

There is little likelihood that the intense specialization of PhD graduate programmes will change much, and indeed perhaps in some fields it should not, lest research competence suffers. Most graduate faculties appear to have reached that conclusion but at the same time are now more conscious than in earlier periods of the need to prepare doctoral students for teaching.

Appointment procedures

Before the 1960s faculty candidates were identified through letters of inquiry to doctoral granting departments, leaders in the discipline and professional friends in other universities. It was considered bad form to advertise vacancies. The civil rights laws and affirmative action, instituted by the federal government in the 1960s to ensure that minorities and women are given equal opportunity for positions, changed the procedures. Virtually every academic vacancy is now advertised, usually in one or more national journals of the discipline or in the *Chronicle of Higher Education*, a national weekly newspaper.

While faculty search, recruitment and appointment procedures vary among institutions and types of institution, most universities and some colleges follow essentially the same process. The department chairman appoints a committee of faculty to conduct the search and recommend candidates. The position is advertised in appropriate publications and announcement of the vacancy is sent to leading graduate departments. Anyone who is interested submits a letter of application along with a résumé of training, professional experience, other qualifications and list of references. Junior faculty and new recipients of the doctorate usually have references on file at the placement service of the institution where they received the doctorate, letters of recommendation from supervisors where they have worked and from professors which can be posted to the institution to which they are applying. This relieves faculty and others of having to write multiple letters of recommendation.

The search committee selects from the applicants those who show most promise for further investigation. If the national or a regional meeting of the field of study concerned occurs during the search process, one or two members of the committee will attend and interview candidates who have applied.

Written letters of recommendation are of limited value. Most states have open record laws which cause letter writers to refrain from candour. For this and other reasons, committee members usually telephone several individuals who know each candidate on the short list, often including some not listed by the candidate. Members of the committee are also likely to go to a library and read each candidate's journal publications to assess scholarly skills.

After each candidate on the short list is considered, the list is reduced to three to five persons who are usually brought to the campus for interview, if funds permit. If the department lacks funds it may bring only two candidates to the campus. For institutions in the east and mid-west, where most of the leading graduate institutions are located, the expense is not great, but for institutions in the west and south-west the distances are great and the cost considerable.

During the visit the candidate will probably be interviewed by the search committee on more than one occasion and at some length and by the department chairman, other faculty in the department, the dean of the school or college, and will usually meet a group of students. The candidate may also be asked to present a lecture on a topic of his choice before the faculty and students in the department. In a smaller university or college the candidate will also be interviewed by the chief academic officer and possibly by the president.

After all candidates have been interviewed the search committee presents its recommendation to the department chairman who may submit it to the vote of the entire faculty of the department. The chairman then forwards the department's recommendation to the college dean who decides whether to authorize an offer. In smaller institutions the final decision is made by the chief academic officer or sometimes by the president.

With the foregoing approval the department chairman negotiates with the nominee by telephone concerning salary, rank, moving expenses and other conditions. In the case of a senior faculty member negotiation might include the question of reduced teaching load to allow more time for research, laboratory space and equipment, secretarial service and student assistants, research funds, costs of additional trips to look for housing, and tenure if it is not automatic for the rank offered.

In leading research universities very prestigious senior faculty may negotiate employment for the spouse, time for outside consulting or employment beyond that provided in university policy, and authority to employ one or more junior faculty to assist with research.

Procedures for the appointment of senior faculty differ from those in recruiting junior faculty in several other ways. Often senior faculty will not apply but are recommended by others and sought by the search committee. Sometimes committee members visit the candidate on his campus first, to persuade him to become a candidate. When he visits the campus it may be primarily to determine whether he wishes to move rather than to persuade the institution to offer the position, since he is being sought rather than seeking the position.

Evaluation

After a faculty member has been appointed he is evaluated periodically for several purposes. All faculty, tenured and untenured, are evaluated annually for purposes of compensation. This may consist of only summary judgment by the department chairman and dean or it may involve formal evaluation by a committee of senior faculty.

The major evaluations for an assistant professor involve annual or triennial evaluations for retention, then evaluation for tenure and, either then or later, for promotion to associate professor. The criteria for each are the same — teaching, research and service — with some variation in emphasis at different stages. Before earning tenure, when the individual is being evaluated to determine retention emphasis is on teaching and research, with less attention to service. Some assistant professors prove to be ineffective teachers and are terminated for that reason, but in universities failure to show promise in research is more likely to be a barrier to tenure. Publication alone is not sufficient; in most fields the individual must have published results of research in refereed journals, that is, journals that use panels of scholars selected nationally to choose articles for publication, in contrast to those in which the editor alone selects articles to publish.

In some fields, for example, history, in leading universities a faculty member must have published a scholarly book to qualify for promotion to full professor. In the sciences it is usually difficult to earn promotion to full professor without having demonstrated the ability to prepare research proposals that will secure funding from federal research agencies or other sources. Promotion from associate professor to full professor also involves higher expectations in the service role.

The most common methods of assessing a faculty member's teaching are quite indirect — hearsay from students and other faculty members, conversations with the teacher and other informal means. Most institutions have tried to increase their objectivity through use of written student evaluations of faculty members' teaching, through visits to classes by senior faculty or administrators (somewhat rare in leading universities, more common in private liberal arts colleges, community colleges and small state institutions), examination of syllabuses and other teaching materials by the chairman or committee, reports from former students, and occasionally other approaches. Increasingly institutions are requiring faculty to submit annual reports documenting their professional activities, which serve partly as a basis for evaluation.

Many senior faculty and administrators insist that despite its apparent drawbacks the indirect approach is effective in assessing a faculty member's teaching performance, as effective as more formal, time-consuming measures. This is particularly true in small institutions where administrators and senior faculty are more aware of junior faculty members' work.

Each year or at other appropriate times a committee of senior faculty is appointed by the department chairman to evaluate faculty being considered for retention, tenure or promotion, and is provided with a documentary file of each faculty member's professional performance. A decision to retain the faculty member before granting tenure is made by the department chairman, upon recommendation of the committee and subject to nominal review by higher authority. A recommendation to terminate must usually have the approval of the dean of the college and perhaps the central administration. A recommendation for awarding tenure or promotion must be approved by the president of the university, based on recommendations by the department committee and chairman, the dean of the college or school and the chief academic officer of the institution, and in many institutions must be approved by the board of trustees.

In reviewing recommendations for tenure and promotion it is the task of the dean to ensure that all departments in the college apply minimally acceptable standards in their recommendations and the chief academic officer assumes the same role for the institution as a whole.

When an untenured faculty member is to be terminated the department chairman usually informs him in writing by 1 March, if he is in his first year in a tenure track position at that institution, or 1 December if he is in his second year; after two years he must be given a full year's notice. While the long period of advance notice is humane and necessary it leads to problems; some faculty members feel they should not have been terminated and after being notified do not perform as effectively and responsibly as they should. A few become disruptive and obstructionist.

Evaluation of senior faculty tends to be perfunctory and often informal. A few institutions conduct formal evaluations of tenured faculty every five years. Feedback from the committee provides the faculty member with information on which to base improvement of his performance; in addition the act of formal evaluation and the knowledge of it among colleagues serves as a stimulus to faculty members to examine their work and to make needed changes.

Compensation

Most faculty are appointed for the academic year — 1 September to 31 May — although some contracts define the period as ten months, with time for vacation allowed in the contract period. Faculty who teach or conduct research in the summer are paid additionally. The rate of pay for summer work varies among institutions, from a maximum of three-ninths or two-tenths additional to a variety of flat rates. Some flat rates differ among ranks while others are the same for all ranks. In some public institutions state funding is provided for instruction in the academic year, but summer course offerings must be self-supporting, that is, tuition fees must be sufficient to pay faculty salaries for summer teaching.

Many faculty devote their entire summer to research with funding from outside the institution — a federal agency, private industry, a foundation or some other source. Such activity is common in engineering, the natural sciences and the health sciences, and to a somewhat lesser extent in business administration and the social sciences including economics and psychology. In the humanities, fine arts and education only a small percentage of faculty is likely to have outside funding for research in the summer; on the other hand the percentage of these faculty needed for summer teaching is usually higher. A few faculty who can afford it voluntarily choose not to teach or conduct funded research in the summer but use the time to travel, write or find a mountain retreat and read.

In some institutions department chairmen are appointed on a twelve-months basis whether they teach or not, but most teach in the summer, at least part-time. In land-grant universities most professors in colleges of agriculture are appointed on a twelve-months basis with part of the time budgeted for research during the academic year and all or part for research in the summer. Faculty in medical schools and dental schools are usually appointed on a twelve-months basis, although they offer no courses in the summer but do research and clinical service.

Salaries vary widely in American higher education. Except for community colleges, most institutions do not have salary scales. Some have a stated minimum for each rank but it is likely to be considerably below almost all salaries. Salaries are based primarily on what the institution can afford to pay and competition in the marketplace. In fields of study where the supply of PhD degree holders is short salaries are much higher; hence a beginning PhD assistant professor in history might have been paid $20 000 per academic year in the mid-1980s while a beginning PhD in accounting or engineering might have been paid $30 000. In general beginning faculty in the humanities are paid less well than those in engineering and business and in some fields of science.

Faculty in law are paid higher salaries and faculty in medicine are paid two to four times as much as faculty in liberal arts, although most medical faculty conduct clinical practice either in the medical school or outside the institution. In some medical schools faculty are allowed to earn an amount equal to their salaries from patients who come to their offices in the teaching hospital; in others all patient fees go into a common fund which is used to supplement salaries. A beginning faculty member in a medical school may be paid $50 000 to $60 000 a year and the most senior faculty may be paid $90 000 to $125 000 per year.

In the most impecunious private colleges beginning faculty may be paid as little as $10 000 per year and senior faculty may be paid less than $20 000 per year. In leading prestige universities $30 000 per year (nine months) is not uncommon for a beginning assistant professor in a discipline in which faculty are scarce, and salaries for full professors usually range from $35 000, except for isolated instances, to $60 000 or $70 000, and in special cases such as chairholders or 'academic stars' as much as $100 000 per year, although such stars are frequently on twelve-month appointment. But these are atypical.

112

Following are average (nine months) salaries, by rank, for the various types of institutions, 1985–6 (*CHE*, 23 April 1986):

Institutions	Professor	Associate professor	Assistant professor
Doctoral	$47 280	$34 040	$28 460
Comprehensive	39 740	31 550	25 930
Baccalaureate	34 280	27 600	22 980
Specialized	40 280	32 050	26 250
Two-year	34 560	29 490	25 140
All types combined	$42 500	$31 800	$26 240

Only two-year institutions with academic rank are included; approximately half the two-year colleges did not have differentiated academic rank.

In institutions that follow the star system, a limited number of professors are paid very high salaries in order to attract them but most of the faculty are paid considerably less. It is assumed that a few stars will attract other outstanding faculty and talented students. This occurs more often in institutions with limited resources, where the institutions are unable to pay top salaries for all faculty. It is usually opposed by the remainder of the faculty who are paid less well, although some argue that the star system improves the institution and in the long run everyone benefits.

Fringe benefits

In addition to salary all institutions provide a variety of non-salary benefits. All faculty participate in the federal government's Old Age and Survivor's Insurance Program, better known as social security, which provides a small income upon retirement for all who have contributed to the programme for a minimum period.

At the end of the last century few colleges provided pension plans for faculty. To remedy that, Andrew Carnegie, the steel magnate, donated $10 million in 1905 to establish a pension fund for college teachers, known as Teachers' Insurance and Annuity Association (TIAA), which invests in interest-bearing securities. Later it added a companion fund known as College Retirement Equities Fund (CREF) which invests in equities, mainly common stocks. About 1500 colleges and universities now participate in the TIAA-CREF pension funds.

In a few states public college and university teachers are required to participate in state retirement programmes, along with all other state employees. In others they are given the option of particpating in the state retirement programme, in TIAA-CREF or in one of dozens of annuity programmes offered by private insurance companies. In virtually all colleges and universities both faculty members and other employees contribute to their pension fund and the institution also contributes, usually an amount equal to the employee contribution but often more.

Other benefits include medical insurance and dental insurance for the employee and his family, insurance for income in case of disability, life insurance and various other types of insurance. In most cases the institution pays all or a portion of the cost of insurance or arranges for its availability at lower cost.

Many private colleges and universities provide free tuition for the faculty member's spouse and children plus free or reduced charges for admission to most activities of the college or university. A small percentage of private institutions provide free housing for faculty and their families, particularly for faculty whose duties make on-campus housing desirable.

Faculty support

The amount of financial support provided by institutions for expenses related to teaching and research varies widely, especially in private institutions. Private colleges and universities with large endowments provide ample secretarial service, office space, laboratories and research equipment, teaching and research supplies and computer time, and fill virtually all requests for books and other library and teaching materials. On the other hand in many of the poorest private colleges little or no secretarial service is provided, no private telephone, often several faculty share an office, there is limited laboratory equipment, no funds for research, none for travel and very little for library materials. Based on funding we would rate these institutions as failures, yet many of them do a very satisfactory job of providing their students with an education, due primarily to faculty dedication, hard work and close personal attention to students.

Public institutions are somewhere between these two examples. Most receive enough funds from state governments to meet minimum requirements but none receives enough to meet all teaching and research needs. Since a portion of their funds usually comes from local taxes public community colleges are sometimes better provided with operating expenses than state universities.

No institution has developed significant research programmes with institutional funds alone; all rely largely on grants and contacts from outside the institution to finance research. Departments that are able to secure research grants are better able to afford the amenities as well as the necessities for teaching and research. As a consequence the humanities, fine arts, education, and social sciences enjoy less support for operations than engineering, the natural sciences, business administration, the health sciences and other fields of study that can attract grants and contracts.

Faculty development

Most institutions encourage faculty to attend national and regional meetings of their disciplines and provide at least a portion of the funds required for travel. Few institutions are able to cover all expenses for all faculty attending such meetings. Many faculty pay travel costs from research grants when the purpose of the conference and the grant coincide, but faculty without such outside support usually pay a portion of their costs of attending professional conferences from personal funds. Departments with limited funds often reserve them for faculty who are invited to present papers at scientific and scholarly conferences or who are officers or committee members of the organization.

Between a half and three-quarters of institutions provide for sabbatical leave with at least half pay (Centra, 1976). Although sabbatical leave policies vary among institutions, most allow faculty such leave once every seven years for one semester with half pay or, in many institutions, an option of one year with half pay or one semester with full pay. Sabbatical leave is not automatic. The faculty member must present a proposal indicating how the time will be used — further study, research, writing, and so on — and secure institutional approval. In addition many institutions place a limit on the number of faculty who may be on sabbatical leave at one time, usually not more than 3 to 5 per cent.

Approximately a quarter of the institutions provide for lighter teaching loads for first-year faculty, and a substantial portion provide for course load reductions to allow a faculty member to develop a new course or make major revisions. To the extent that funds are available, more than half the colleges and universities provide full or part-time employment in the summer to permit a few faculty to develop new courses or improve them.

Awards for teaching excellence have been developed on many campuses in recent years; in the mid-1970s, 79 per cent of the universities, 44 per cent of the four-year colleges and 20 per cent of the community colleges had such programmes (Centra, 1976).

Participation in governance

As pointed out in Chapter 2 faculty members are sometimes found on governing boards of institutions, rarely on the boards of their own institutions in the case of public colleges and universities, somewhat more commonly on governing boards of their own institutions in the private sector and most commonly on boards of institutions where they are not employed. Faculty participation in institutional decisions occurs most commonly through internal governance structures rather than membership of the board of trustees.

The major avenue for faculty participation in decision making on most campuses is the faculty senate, often called academic senate, especially when it includes others in addition to faculty. Faculty representatives to the senate are elected by colleges and schools within the institution. In some institutions the faculty senate is composed solely of faculty; in others the senate consists of both faculty and a designated number of administrators, often serving by virtue of their positions. In the latter case administrators serving in the senate ex-officio usually include the president, vice presidents, deans of colleges and other selected administrators, for example, registrar, university attorney, comptroller, and director of externally funded research. Since the 1960s many faculty senates have included student representatives.

Joint faculty-administrative senates usually foster closer working relationships between faculty and administration; separate jurisdictions tend to lead to confrontation more readily.

The extent of faculty influence on institutional policy-making through its faculty senate tends to correlate with the prestige of the institution. In the leading research universities the faculty senate usually enjoys a great deal of authority and control over institutional policies. In small, non-prestigious institutions the faculty senate may purport to occupy an influential role but in fact may have little power. Some institutions specify that their faculty senates are authorized to make final decisions on a number of categories, but in most institutions the faculty senate is advisory to the university administration, according to the institution's governance scheme, while in fact the recommendations of the faculty senate are usually, if not always, routinely approved by the university administration. Administrative approval of faculty senate decisions tends to be more routine in joint senates, in which representatives of the administration participate in senate decisions.

Typically senates are expected to decide or to have major voice in decisions on such matters as curricula, degree requirements, scholastic standards, student behaviour and other matters related to teaching and research. In addition, when the faculty are not unionized, senates usually concern themselves with matters related to faculty welfare and privileges — compensation, workload, sabbatical leaves, fringe benefits, and so on — which administrators examine more critically and may not routinely approve.

Typically academic senates function through a number of standing and special committees whose chairmen are usually elected members of the senate but whose members may include faculty who are not elected members of the senate. In the early 1970s the University of Minnesota had twenty-two standing committees of the senate, and the senate of the University of California at Berkeley had thirty-two standing committees. At one time the University of Maryland faculty senate had twenty-seven standing and special committees, averaging eighteen members per committee, which meant that approximately one out of five of its faculty served on a senate committee each year. Committees investigate matters brought to their attention, hold hearings on controversial issues, accumulate evidence and make recommendations to the senate as a whole. In very large universities the senate often does its work primarily through the committee structure with the senate itself routinely approving most committee recommendations while at the same time retaining veto power.

Further faculty participation in governance takes place within the college or school of each institution through a college assembly of all faculty members in the college or a college council composed of representatives of departments which study and recommend policies for the college and often policies that are recommended to the senate of the institution.

In most institutions faculty members in departments participate directly in departmental faculty meetings and in all decisions taken by the department, but in very large departments, for example, more than fifty faculty members, there is often an executive committee of five to ten elected members who meet frequently and take appropriate action, bringing to the entire departmental faculty only certain categories of policy issues. Typically the executive committee members are senior faculty with long tenure at the institution.

Faculty unions

Three unions serve faculty in American higher education: the American Federation of Teachers (AFT), an affiliate of the American Federation of Labor-Congress of Industrial Organizations (AFL-CIO), the principal labour organization in the US; the National Education Association (NEA); and the American Association of University Professors (AAUP).

The AFT and the NEA serve primarily elementary and secondary school teachers; the AAUP serves only college and university faculty.

Public elementary and secondary school teachers were the first teachers to be unionized — by the AFT in the 1950s. The NEA was a long-established professional association of elementary and secondary school teachers, staff and administrators, with a division for members in higher education, primarily teacher education faculty. As the AFT began to attract members from the NEA in the early 1960s, the latter organization felt increasing pressure from some of its members to unionize and in 1963 declared itself a collective bargaining agency.

The AAUP, originally founded in 1915 to protect academic freedom of college and university faculty members, was the last of the three to include collective bargaining among its functions. The AAUP saw the AFT and NEA attracting AAUP members who desired to have union representation and felt it could stop the loss if it became a collective bargaining agency.

In addition to serving as collective bargaining agent in institutions in states where public employee unions are legal, AAUP chapters at institutions in other states continue to assume the same role the national organization did before becoming involved in union activities. When AAUP became a collective bargaining agent many of the older, more distinguished scholars and scientists resigned, individuals who did not want to be associated with a union. With some chapters serving as bargaining agents and others not, the AAUP has difficulty with its identity.

Twenty-six states have passed laws permitting college and university faculty to bargain collectively and while there are local union chapters on some campuses in states that do not permit collective bargaining by public employees, they tend to be small and not very effective. Except for two specialized institutions, the first institutional faculties to unionize were the eighteen institutions of the City University of New York in 1969.

By the end of 1985, 850 colleges and universities were unionized, approximately 25 per cent of the institutions in the country (*CHE*, 19 March 1986). The largest number of unionized institutions is found among two-year colleges and the smallest number among private institutions (*CHE*, 8 May 1985).

Unionization of private institutions was slowed by a case concerning Yeshiva University in New York City in which the court ruled that since the faculty was empowered to make many decisions of a managerial nature, under federal law the faculty was a part of management and therefore unable to bargain collectively. This was reinforced a few years later when the National Labor Relations Board ruled that the faculty union at Boston University could not bargain collectively since the faculty had major managerial authority.

None of the leading universities has unionized faculties. For example, of the fifty-six members of the Association of American Universities, the leading graduate institutions in the country, none is unionized, although referendums have been held at several of them.

At leading universities not only are salaries and working conditions better but faculty generally have more influence in institutional decision-making and have less need for unions. In addition some faculty feel that the pressure strategies of unions are inappropriate in an intellectual environment where logic, reason and persuasion have historically provided the basis for decision-making. The behaviour of some faculty union leaders, particularly during strikes, has offended many academics who place high value on civilities.

Many academics have been and continue to be fearful that the presence of a collective bargaining unit (union) on a campus will diminish collegiality and the role of the academic senate, and that its functions will be supplanted by the union leadership who will bargain with the administration on matters usually considered by the senate. Many matters formerly dealt with by the academic senate are indeed handled by the union leadership on campuses that have collective bargaining but unions have not replaced academic senates completely. In fact in some institutions the role of the senate has been enhanced because its privileges and spheres of responsibility are specified in the union's bargaining agreement with the institution. This is particularly the case in institutions in which the unions restrict their concerns to salaries and working conditions and leave to the academic senate responsibility for deciding academic matters — degrees, courses, curricula, standards, calendar, student life, promotion, tenure and other academic matters.

Outside employment

Consulting for business, industry and governmental agencies is a major activity of faculty in some fields of study and a major source of supplementary income. Faculty in business administration are called on for consultation more than those in other fields of study, followed closely by engineering faculty. Faculty in law, economics, medicine, computer science, geology and, in varying degrees, other sciences engage in outside consulting. There are fewer opportunities for faculty in other fields but in most leading universities faculty in all the social sciences, education and most other fields engage in consulting to some extent.

Most studies of consulting have found that nationally about 40 per cent of faculty engage in consulting for pay to some extent in a typical year and another 20 per cent provide consultation assistance without pay, usually to foundations, religious groups and other non-profit organizations. Of those who do consulting, approximately 20 per cent devote more than half a day per week, on average; 5 per cent devote more than one day per week.

Why do universities encourage faculty members to serve as consultants to business, industry, government and other organizations outside the university? The primary benefit is the information brought to the classroom, observations about current practice that enhance the quality of teaching. It also contributes to the professor's research, provides a needed service that builds goodwill and support for the university, helps the faculty member to stay current in his field and gives him more credibility with students and those who employ university graduates, contributes to the prestige of the university thereby enhancing employment opportunities for its graduates and in many cases makes it possible for the university to employ a faculty member for whom the university salary alone would not be adequate attraction. Although, on average, consulting accounts for only about 15 per cent of the earnings of the faculty members who consult, for a small percentage it is a major source of income and for a very few income from consulting exceeds their university salaries.

There are many criticisms of consulting, growing out of abuses of the consulting privilege accorded faculty members; however most studies of faculty consulting have found that those who consult carry teaching loads equal to those who do not consult, publish more, and are as involved in university governance activities.

Second jobs

Regular employment in a second job is not a usual practice but is not rare, particularly among faculty in community colleges and in institutions in large cities. If second jobs are in the evenings or at weekends most institutions do not monitor or regulate them although some take the position that any imposition on a faculty member's time reduces his effectiveness as a teacher and researcher and either prohibit second jobs or set conditions in which they may be held.

Private practice

Many faculty members engage in private practice of their professions outside the university on a part-time basis. This is common among clinical psychologists and others who set up private practices in counselling for emotional problems, marriage counselling, alcoholism and other personal problems. Engineers, chemists and physicists occasionally establish testing laboratories which are operated by employees but managed by the faculty member on a part-time basis.

120

In addition to consulting, a few law faculty are employed by law firms on a part-time basis, usually in an advisory capacity although they may occasionally appear in court to represent a client. And some particularly talented law professors are well known for their representation of clients in particularly difficult cases; some earn fees several times their university salaries.

Most faculty members in schools of medicine conduct private practice; it is considered necessary to maintain their skills in their specialty. Some have offices away from the school. Others are allowed offices for private practice in the medical school; as noted earlier, they are often permitted to earn income equal to their university salary. In other cases, however, income from private practice goes to the university, which uses it to supplement the physician's state-funded salary.

Other teaching

Most colleges and universities operate extension or continuing education programmes which are self-supporting, and administratively separate from the central academic enterprise, offering both credit courses, that is, those that apply towards an academic degree, and non-credit courses, mostly in the evenings and at weekends. Most institutions have policies permitting faculty members to teach in such programmes or in nearby institutions but with a limit on the amount of time that may be thus spent or the amount of income that may be earned in this way.

Few colleges or universities pay overtime in connection with a faculty member's principal responsibilities; however a few institutions, particularly community colleges and unionized institutions, provide for overtime pay for faculty who perform certain extra duties or carry larger than required teaching loads.

Faculty in government service

The federal government relies heavily on university faculty for advice and consultation on a wide range of topics. Research grants by the National Institutes of Health, the National Science Foundation, and other agencies of the federal government that provide research funds, use panels of university professors to judge applications for research. This type of service usually pays no salary, only expenses. In addition many government agencies and committees of Congress call on university professors for advice on matters of public policy.

When a new administration takes office in Washington it is faced with a task of filling hundreds of non-Civil Service administrative positions. Every administration turns to the universities to fill many of these positions. This practice first became common in the administration of Franklin D. Roosevelt when he became President in 1933; he brought into the government a large number of professors, mostly from universities in the north-east. Every President since has followed the practice. Most of these faculty stay in government a few years and then return to academe. Very few remain permanently in government service; nor do all of them return to university posts. When Democrats are out of power some of these faculty, especially economists, take positions with the Brookings Institution, a liberal 'think tank' in Washington, and when the Republicans are out of office some of the academics in the administration take positions with the American Enterprise Institute, a conservative 'think tank', also in Washington.

The number of professors who seek elective office is small but in each election several are elected to the Congress. The only professor to become President of the United States was Woodrow Wilson, in 1913, who had previously served as Governor of the State of New Jersey and President of Princeton University. Positions in the federal government and the US Congress require full-time service and do not permit professors or others to retain their non-governmental positions while in government service.

Some faculty members are elected to state legislatures but the number is small because legislative service is a part-time position; legislatures meet for only a few months each year or, in some states, a few months every two years. Most faculty members cannot arrange to be away from their teaching posts for several months each year or every other year and salaries for legislative service alone do not provide adequate income to support them.

Faculty mobility

During the 1960s when college and university enrolments were expanding rapidly and there was a shortage of faculty in most fields of study, faculty movement from one campus to another was frequent. Beginning in the 1970s, when the supply of PhD trained faculty in most fields equalled or exceeded demand, the amount of such movement slowed markedly. In fields in which there is a shortage of PhD trained faculty a high level of mobility continues but not in most fields. There is one exception. The supply of faculty has led to an increase in the number of assistant professors who fail to gain tenure and must move, but among tenured faculty fewer opportunities to move occur. This is not to suggest that movement of faculty among institutions has ceased; there are still vacancies created by resignations, death or retirement, and some institutions, particularly community colleges, continue to grow and add faculty.

Many institutions recruit academic administrators from more prestigious campuses; thus a leading professor at a research university might become a dean, vice president or president at a comprehensive university. The reverse, that is, to move from a faculty position in a comprehensive university to an administrative position in a leading research university, is unusual.

Movement of faculty to positions outside higher education is common, particularly in the applied fields. Faculty in business administration, engineering, law, geological sciences, economics, medicine and other health sciences find opportunities in private business or private practice. In most cases their income increases substantially. The academic world is a prime source of staff leadership for non-profit foundations, trade associations, professional organizations and government.

Appointment of individuals from business, industry and other non-university sectors to faculty positions occurs less frequently but is not uncommon, especially in fields where practical experience is valued, such as law, medicine, dentistry, business administration and engineering. Several schools of business have appointed as deans individuals who have been highly successful in business but lacked academic credentials.

Academic subcultures

Every profession can be characterized by a set of values peculiar to that profession. This is particularly true for physicians, lawyers, policemen, the clergy and certain other professions. It is also true among college and university faculty even though, as a profession, they are less monolithic than some others.

The right of a faculty member to teach according to his understanding of the research evidence, and conduct research and publish findings without fear of retribution from those who disagree is universally accepted among faculty in America and other countries. Yet there are many areas of disagreement and differences among faculty.

Politics

Like academics in other countries, American faculty are more liberal as a group than society as a whole; but there are wide differences related to the type of institution, geography, subject, race, religion, quantity and quality of education, and so on. Among religious groups, Jewish faculty are by far the most liberal; Catholic and Protestant faculty are predominantly liberal, Catholics more so by a small margin.

Among institutions, faculty in élite private universities and selective liberal arts colleges are the most liberal and faculty in small state colleges and community colleges are the most conservative, excepting colleges sponsored by fundamentalist church denominations.

Black faculty vote for candidates of the Democratic party by a wide margin; so do Hispanic faculty, by a somewhat smaller margin. The most liberal to the most conservative faculty by discipline are: social work, social sciences, humanities, fine arts, medicine, physical sciences, biological sciences, education, business administration, engineering, nursing, home economics and agriculture (Ladd and Lipset, 1975).

Geographically faculty in the north-east are the most liberal, along with those on the west coast, followed by the middle west, with those in the south and south-west most conservative. Faculty who live in larger cities tend to be more liberal than those who live in rural areas.

Social differentiation

Generalizations about faculty must be tempered by the fact that there are great differences among faculty, individually and collectively. A professor of Sanskrit at an élite private university in Boston and a professor of agronomy in a small state college in North Dakota have little in common. The settings in which they work and the people with whom they interact vary widely. The professor of Sanskrit is likely to spend much of his day in the library examining ancient documents, interrupted by luncheon at the campus faculty club where the conversation is urbane and about world affairs. The professor of agronomy may spend much of his day supervising the planting of experimental crops, interrupted by lunch at the Rotary Club in the local town where conversation centres on the weather and prospects for crop production.

One of the criticisms of American universities is that faculty members of different disciplines associate with one another so little. On a large university campus faculty members are likely to associate with others within their own college or even department to the exclusion of other faculty on campus; this tends to be more common among faculty in business administration, engineering and other applied fields. Many faculty know almost no faculty in other colleges of the university and sometimes few or none in other departments within their own college, except those they meet while serving in the faculty senate or on university or college committees. Mutual professional or disciplinary interests tend to provide the basis for social groupings.

A sociologist who studied faculty several years ago in a large research university and a regional state college characterized the two as 'cosmopolitans and locals' (Gouldner, 1958). Almost all the faculty in the research university held the doctorate, were discipline oriented, communicated with scholars or scientists in their fields of study nationally and identified with the university where they worked and the town and state in which it was located in only a very limited way. At the small state college less than half the faculty held the doctorate, they knew few people in their fields of study nationally, spent little time in research and identified strongly with the college, the town and the state where they worked. They participated in community activities and many of their friends were townspeople not associated with the college, in contrast to the university faculty who associated primarily with other university faculty and knew fewer non-university towns-people. There are many individual exceptions to these two profiles, individual faculty members and institutions that do not fit either, but to a considerable degree it is still valid although the differences are less distinct. One major exception is that most of the faculty in the state college now hold the doctorate and because of their education are less different from their university colleagues.

In their national survey of faculty, Ladd and Lipset found that faculty in high prestige institutions were more likely to have had fathers who were professionals or managers, and faculty in low prestige institutions were more likely to have had fathers who were labourers or skilled workers. They also found that faculty participated in cultural activities more than the general populace but attended church less. Some 27 per cent of faculty went to a concert once a month, and another 51 per cent went more than a few times a year. Some 22 per cent saw a play once a month plus another 56 per cent a few times a year. Approximately 42 per cent of faculty reported that they rarely or never went to church, and 40 per cent never attended sports events.

Attitudes towards faculty unionism were mixed. Conservative faculty tended to be less positive towards unions. On the other hand unionism was found most in low prestige institutions. Faculty who saw themselves primarily as teachers were more positive towards faculty unions than those who saw themselves as researchers, although the latter tended to be more liberal than the former.

In terms of religion a disproportionately larger percentage of Jews were found in the more prestigious institutions, while more Catholics were found in lower prestige institutions; the latter is accounted for, at least in part, by the fact that a large number of private liberal arts colleges are operated by the Catholic Church.

Titles

There is wide variation among American institutions and individual faculty in the use of the academic titles 'professor' and 'doctor'. In less distinguished colleges and universities, especially in which a minority of the faculty hold the doctorate, the title 'doctor' is often emphasized. At the other extreme in the most prestigious universities, where it is assumed that everyone holds the doctorate or is a person of significant academic achievement, the title doctor is rarely used among colleagues. Different institutions adopt different modes of address. In the most prestigious institutions faculty are usually addressed by the title 'professor', regardless which of the three professorial ranks they hold. At a few élite universities faculty address one another as 'Mr' and the use of the title doctor or professor is considered gauche; on the other hand, some consider this a form of reverse snobbery.

When a person without an academic background enters the university as a teacher or administrator, he occasionally finds lack of a doctoral degree a social or academic handicap and he or his friends are likely to arrange for an honorary doctorate to be bestowed on him. Conversely some faculty of high achievement reject honorary doctorates as irrelevant. A noted professor at Harvard, a scholar of international reputation and author of many books, who had an LL.B degree but no doctorate, reputedly spurned all efforts to bestow a doctorate on him. His fame and prestige made the doctorate unimportant and he enjoyed being one of the very few Harvard faculty who did not hold the doctorate.

Prestige

While there are no formal class differences in American higher education, there are many kinds of differentiation based on institutional type and quality, discipline, role, and so on. Many of these differences are subtle and not evident to the visitor or non-academic. If leading academicians were asked to list the hundred top universities in rank order there would be considerable agreement in their listings. The large research universities rank at the top with the élite highly selective private liberal arts colleges in a high but separate category. At the bottom are the small state colleges, formerly teacher's colleges, and the small private non-selective liberal arts colleges, Bible colleges and other special institutions not known for superior intellectual activity. In a separate category but below these are the community colleges and two-year vocational-technical schools.

Those who study academic institutions often determine prestige according to selectivity in student admissions, credentials of faculty, volumes in library, publications by faculty, faculty service on national commissions and other bodies, size of endowment, national awards received by students and graduates, expenditures per student, student/faculty ratio, and so on.

Discipline is a basis of considerable differentiation. In medicine, for example, neuro-surgeons rank at or near the top in prestige while general practitioners are near the bottom. The experimental psychologist considers himself the élite of that discipline and regards the counselling psychologist as a lesser scholar. In a national ranking of all disciplines classics or physics usually ranks first and home economics last, raising a question about the relationship between prestige of a discipline and its social utilty.

Efforts to rank colleges and universities according to the quality of academic programmes is a topic of intense disagreement among American academics. The first such major effort was in 1964 when the American Council on Education surveyed thousands of faculty members to identify their ratings of the quality of graduate programmes in twenty-nine fields of study in the arts and sciences and engineering. From this survey the leading universities in each of the fields were identified and, while faculty in those institutions were gratified, in many other universities faculty were disappointed and felt that the procedure was biased. Since that time several such surveys have been conducted and other disciplines have been added. Lists of leading graduate programmes are criticized as being popularity polls, yet few academics ignore them. All the surveys are based on research productivity of the faculty; they reveal little about the teaching programme. No comparable rating of undergraduate programmes exists.

The college professor, as depicted in American movies a generation ago, was seen as a dedicated scholar immersed in books and largely unaware of the world about him. Poorly paid, he lived in modest circumstances and found his pleasures in books and classical music. This image is no longer accurate, if it ever was.

Today's faculty member is usually well informed about world and national affairs, is probably an avid reader of a wide variety of publications and watches much of the same television as other people, excepting a small percentage who eschew television or limit their watching to the Public Broadcasting channel. He is likely to be an investor in the stock market and knowledgable about current interest rates. He has travelled extensively in the US and has probably been abroad, most likely to western Europe.

Most of the changes among faculty occurred as a result of the vast influx of new teachers entering the profession during the explosion of enrolments in the 1960s and 1970s. The new teachers were influenced by the values of the period and while they adopted most of the values of academe they also brought changes that have permeated all through higher education — consulting, unionism, demand for reasonable salaries, demand for more voice in institutional affairs, less deference to tradition, familiar relationships with one another and with students and many more.

Note

1   The term 'faculty' refers to teachers as a group, rather than a division of a university, as in Europe.

6 Teaching

In highly selective colleges and universities undergraduate students are fairly homogeneous intellectually and capable of dealing with college level material easily. In less selective institutions teachers encounter a more difficult task; within a single class are highly talented students and others whose ability to handle college work is marginal. The widest range of academic ability is found in community colleges where, due to the open admissions policy followed by most, classes include students with high academic ability together with a few who can barely read and write.

Most faculty seek an objective level of student achievement but are inevitably faced with and influenced by the competence of students who enrol. In open admissions colleges and less selective institutions teachers strive to help less talented and less well-prepared students to achieve, while at the same time trying to challenge the more capable students.

In some less selective state colleges and universities as many as a quarter of the freshman class does not return the second year; some have failed academically, others have decided that they should not attend college or that they have chosen the wrong institution or field of study.

In less selective urban institutions, including both community colleges and senior colleges and universities that enrol high percentages of part-time students, it is not unusual for a quarter of the students enrolled in the fall semester not to return for the spring semester. Students who work full-time and attend college part-time may interrupt their studies several times before completing a degree. This lack of continuity presents additional problems for teachers.

Teaching methods

The lecture is the most commonly used teaching technique in American colleges and universities, particularly at the undergraduate level and in large classes. In law almost all of the teaching is by lecture, with limited student recitation. Except for clinical instruction, almost all the teaching in medical and dental schools is by lecture.

In large institutions class size frequently dictates the use of the lecture, although even in the largest universities class size in some fields of study at the junior and senior levels is small enough to permit other approaches. Some faculty prefer lecturing; they say it is the only way they can bring about the kind of student learning they seek, but most prefer discussion. At the graduate level and often at the advanced undergraduate level, the method is a mixture of lecture and student discussion; students are expected to be ready to discuss assigned reading in class.

The number of charismatic lecturers in higher education, the kind who keep students on the edges of their seats throughout every lecture, is small. Most faculty recognize their limitations as lecturers and, if class size permits, introduce as much discussion and student interaction as possible.

In large lecture classes at the freshman and sophomore levels in fields such as history, political science, sociology, psychology and the humanities, it is common for a faculty member to lecture twice a week and for the students to meet in small groups once a week with a graduate teaching assistant who answers questions and leads group discussion.

In liberal arts colleges and other small institutions and departments teaching involves interaction including small seminars, colloquia and work groups. While objective measures of learning do not uniformly favour small classes more than large ones, students prefer smaller classes and feel they learn more and enjoy the educational experience more in them. For these and other reasons many private liberal arts colleges remain small by choice, even if it means turning away highly qualified students who apply for admission.

Independent study includes several different approaches. The most flexible consists of a verbal agreement between student and teacher concerning a topic on which the student will read and write, interspersed with tutorial sessions with the teacher. It also includes research in the laboratory or library in which the student undertakes an investigation in much the same way as for a thesis. Another form of independent study is contract study in which the student writes a plan with the teacher's guidance for studying a given body of knowledge, often comparable to a course which is not offered in the institution and then proceeds according to the contract which the two sign. Evergreen State College in Olympia, Washington, is an experimental institution where a substantial portion of every student's curriculum is composed of contract studies.

Another form of independent study is programmed learning in which the student is provided with a manual and other materials which have been written to take the student through the entire course systematically. It involves mastery learning of each segment or unit before the student proceeds to the next; in addition to programmed texts, it may use teaching machines, computers and learning modules. It requires a large amount of faculty time and its use is limited, partly because many students cannot work effectively alone.

Self-paced instruction (SPI), a variation of programmed learning, known by several names including Personalized System of Instruction, and the Keller Plan, for Professor Fred Keller who popularized the system, was introduced at many colleges and universities in the late 1960s and 1970s. The subject matter of a full course is divided into a large number of units and the student proceeds to master each through independent study interspersed with tutorial instruction; he is not allowed to go on until each unit is mastered, hence it is impossible to reach the end of the course without having mastered the entire course. SPI fits the laboratory sciences best but is also used with almost all undergraduate fields of study. Although faculty see each student only occasionally it consumes an inordinate amount of their time. For students who can discipline themselves it is an effective method of learning. Unfortunately the student usually paces himself, so SPI courses get delayed when they compete with formal courses for the student's time. Variations of this approach are known as auto-tutorial or audio-tutorial instruction.

Teaching technologies

For more than twenty years beginning in the 1950s various technologies materialized for use in teaching and for a period college and university faculty became enthusiastic about them. Many would try them out then in due course the excitement waned and most teaching returned to established methods. Some technologies have endured but not nearly at peak levels of use or near the levels the promoters had anticipated.

Television continues to be used in teaching but it has never gained the acceptance early enthusiasts predicted. Many institutions tried it in the 1950s and 1960s but discontinued it for various reasons; principally they believed that where class meetings were possible they resulted in more effective education. Several institutions produce and broadcast courses; among the leaders are Dallas County (Texas) Community College District which has seven institutions; Miami-Dade (Florida) Community College; and several community colleges in California. The University of Mid-America, a distance learning institution, relies heavily on televised courses, as does a university of the air which the University of Maryland operates on behalf of a consortium of universities. Some television courses are taught via cable channels but many are offered through local stations of the non-profit Public Broadcasting system, usually during daytime hours.

One of the first uses of computers was for programmed instruction, which had already gained some attention through printed materials and the transfer to computers was easy and logical. Computer assisted instruction is used to transmit information to students but some faculty use the computer only to manage instruction, that is, to give instructions for study to students, keep records and administer tests and examinations. Computers are still used for some teaching but not to the extent early enthusiasts predicted.

The teaching machine, an electro-mechanical device first developed at Ohio State University in 1926, was used largely in experiments in learning but did not gain widespread use in teaching.

Auto-tutorial instruction often relies heavily on tape recordings or slide film or a combination of the two. In self-paced instruction the learning guide often includes directions to go to the library or laboratory to view slides or a filmstrip and listen to the taped discussion prepared for the course.

Teaching load

The workload of faculty varies widely among institutions and is affected by many considerations. In general the heaviest teaching loads are found in community colleges where fifteen credits, that is, five courses of three credits each, are fairly common, with a few such institutions requiring eighteen credits per semester. In most liberal arts colleges, particularly the less selective ones, and in comprehensive colleges and universities, twelve credits are the norm, subject to reduction for non-teaching duties. The same applies to some doctoral granting universities but in most doctoral granting public universities the norm is nine credits per semester of undergraduate courses or six credits of graduate teaching. In the most prestigious and wealthy private universities the teaching requirement is often three courses per year, that is, one for one semester and two for the other semester, giving full recognition to the research expectations of faculty. In addition to teaching courses faculty are expected to direct graduate theses and dissertations, direct a few students in independent study, perhaps supervise students engaged in internships, in addition to service activities and research.

Department chairmen normally teach fewer courses; in a small department the chairman might teach one course fewer than other faculty and in very large departments chairmen teach only one course.

As already mentioned (p. 112) professors in colleges of agriculture have a portion of their time budgeted to research and teach part-time. This is also true for faculty who have outside research funds which support a portion of their salaries.

Faculty who hold endowed chairs and whose salaries and expenses are paid entirely from non-university funds may, if they choose, teach no formal courses but devote their full time to research and directing graduate student research; however this is rare: most chairholders prefer to teach at least one course each semester.

Private institutions are free to set teaching loads as they wish, within the limitations of funds and internal considerations. Public institutions must be sensitive to legislatures which occasionally become concerned about faculty teaching loads, usually after reading a newspaper story about a faculty member who has taught little, and either prescribe the teaching load in legislation or require the governing board to establish a requirement. Many laymen, including legislators, who are unacquainted with the amount of preparation required for teaching and who assume that college and university faculty do nothing but teach classes, find it difficult to understand why faculty may teach only nine hours or six hours of graduate level classes per week.

Faculty participation in departmental decision-making, service on committees and other governance activities consumes a large amount of time, which most of them regret but at the same time believe to be essential. Some faculty members, particularly in the sciences, are able to plan their research so that it can continue under the monitoring of graduate students while they are away. In the humanities the nature of the research is usually such that it is not feasible to parcel it out to assistants.

Student-faculty ratio

This refers to the number of full-time equivalent students per full-time equivalent faculty member. In private well-endowed liberal arts colleges this may be as low as ten students per faculty member (10:1) or even as low as 8:1 in a few cases, while in public institutions with large undergraduate enrolments principally in one or two fields, for example, education and business administration, the ratio may be as high as 25:1. In between are the doctoral granting institutions whose student-faculty ratios average 15:1 to 20:1, usually about 17:1 or 18:1.

Averages can be misleading. Within institutions there is wide variation in the student-faculty ratios among fields of study. For example, the student-faculty ratio in undergraduate courses in business administration may be 35:1 while in the same university the ratio for doctoral study in chemistry is 5:1. Schools of nursing, if they wish to become accredited by the association that accredits nursing programmes, may have no more than ten students per clinical faculty member.

Student-faculty ratios have always been larger in the US than in the UK and some other countries and grew during two periods of rapid enrolment growth in American higher education. Immediately after the Second World War enrolments swelled faster than new faculty could be appointed, then declined in the early and mid-1950s. When the post-war baby boom reached college in the early 1960s enrolment swelled again faster than faculty could be appointed and student-faculty ratios increased dramatically. Fifteen years later when the supply of faculty became ample, most legislators, college and university administrators and trustees had become accustomed to large ratios and did not remember the days of lower ratios. In brief they had accepted the higher ratios as normal and felt no need to reduce them. This occurred about the same time as most institutions were experiencing reduction in funding when adjusted for inflation, and few could have decreased student-faculty ratios substantially if they had wanted to.

Registration

At the beginning of each semester and the summer term one or more days are designated for registration. Computers have expedited the process but it is sometimes an unpleasant process for students.

In a large university registration often takes place in the institution's sports arena. Students complete forms indicating courses in which they wish to enrol and secure the signatures of their faculty advisers and/or their college deans; then they wend their way through a maze of desks in the registration arena where they receive cards authorizing them to enrol in each course. Along the way a photograph is taken for an identification card to be posted to the student later, which admits him to many institutional functions and services including borrowing books from the library. If the student lives in college or university housing, he or she receives a room assignment or confirmation of one previously assigned, is issued authorization to use the institution's food service, receives validation of the student's health examination and documentation for several voluntary services such as a permit to park an automobile in campus parking lots and season tickets to sports contests and games. The last stop is payment where a bill that includes tuition, laboratory fees, parking fees, identification card fee, health service fee, housing, food service, sports tickets, and other mandatory and voluntary fees are totalled and collected by the institution's bursar.

Normally lists of students enrolled in each class are obtained from a computer and supplied by the registrar to teachers the first day of class. Every institution allows a brief period following registration, usually about two weeks, for students to make changes in registration, that is, drop courses, add other courses, change sections when more than one section of a course is taught. After that period the student is charged a fee for making changes. Normally when a course is dropped early in the semester, but after the first two weeks, the student will be given a mark (grade) indicating that the course was dropped or that the student withdrew from the institution. When this occurs late in the semester or quarter the mark indicates whether the student was passing or failing the course at the time it was dropped or the student withdrew from the institution. These remain a part of the student's permanent record but usually involve no penalty unless the student was failing the course at the time he or she dropped the course or withdrew from the institution.

Class meetings

Classes are held five days a week, Monday to Friday. Saturday classes are rare, usually graduate level courses for students who are employed full-time. Until recent years most colleges and universities offered classes from 8 a.m. until 5 p.m. and that continues to be the pattern in institutions that enrol only full-time students. Until the Second World War most institutions, public and private, were located in small towns and enrolled few part-time students; however since then most newly established institutions are located in large population centres and a substantial portion of those enrolled are part-time students, especially at the graduate level. To accommodate part-time students, especially graduate students, most institutions located in urban centres now offer evening classes up to 10 p.m.

At the graduate level, especially in the case of evening classes offered for part-time students, a course may meet once a week for two and a half or three hours. As already mentioned, the typical three-credit

135

undergraduate course meets three times a week for one hour (fifty minutes of instruction plus ten minutes to change classes) for one semester or for one and a half hours per class twice a week. In many undergraduate institutions or colleges, class attendance is compulsory but not at the graduate level unless oral contributions in class constitute part of the basis for grading, for example, speech courses, seminars and so on or in laboratory courses.

Tests and examinations

The typical full-time undergraduate student in an American college or university takes four to six courses each semester or quarter and each course involves a number of tests and a final examination. Some courses, especially more advanced courses, may require only a mid-term exam and a final exam. Others, particularly freshman and sophomore courses, are likely to require several tests during the semester in addition to the mid-term and final examinations. Some of the tests are designed primarily for assessing the effectiveness of teaching so that the teacher can make adjustments, corrections or reteach some material.

Handwritten tests constitute the main type of test used, although, due to large numbers of students, objective tests have almost replaced essay tests in most freshman and sophomore courses at large universities. Such tests consist largely of true or false items, multiple choice items in which the student selects one of five possible answers, sentences with blanks missing to be filled in and questions calling for names, places, dates and other objective data. In large universities where beginning courses in political science, history, sociology, psychology, business administration and others have 100, 200 or occasionally 300 or 400 students, marking essay tests is not feasible. Although most faculty agree that objective tests do not measure some of what a student should have learned, especially when not constructed by an expert test maker, their use becomes a necessity.

In small liberal arts colleges and others where classes are small, essay tests are widely used, as they are in advanced undergraduate courses and graduate courses. Almost all tests used by faculty are constructed by the individual teaching the course. In an institution where there are several sections of the same course, faculty are usually free to vary the contents and emphasis as they choose, and each prepares tests and examinations to fit the material covered.

A typical freshman course involves three to five short tests during the semester in addition to mid-term and final exams; the short tests are frequently called quizzes and may require only twenty or thirty minutes. In some courses, such as mathematics and the sciences, some teachers administer brief 'pop quizzes', meaning not announced in advance, to encourage undergraduates to keep current with their study. Courses in freshman English are largely of the essay type, with course enrolments usually under thirty and often under twenty. Oral tests and examinations are rare, except in speech courses, although students on advanced courses will often be called upon to make oral reports in class.

A bachelor's thesis is common in private liberal arts colleges but rare in public colleges and universities, due largely to numbers. Most faculty agree that the bachelor's thesis is highly desirable but except in institutions with a very low student-faculty ratio it is not practical.

Standardized tests constructed by professional testing agencies are used largely for admissions purposes and rarely in connection with courses, except the College Level Examination Program tests discussed earlier (p. 83). The two admissions tests used are the Scholastic Aptitude Test (SAT) and one by the American College Testing (ACT) programme in Iowa City. The SAT is administered by the College Entrance Examination Board, an affiliate of the Educational Testing Service, a private, non-profit enterprise located in Princeton, New Jersey, which prepares the SAT as well as hundreds of other tests for colleges and universities, schools, government and business.

The comprehensive examination at the end of undergraduate study found in many countries is virtually unknown in American higher education, although it is quite common for graduate degrees. Essentially all candidates for the PhD and comparable degrees take a final examination which may include knowledge of the discipline but in many cases only an examination on the dissertation presented, in which case some months earlier the student would have completed a qualifying or comprehensive examination covering the content of his subject.

Beginning faculty report that they feel less competent in preparing tests and examinations than in any other aspect of the teaching role. They have usually had no training in their graduate studies in how to prepare tests unless they took a course in teaching in which case there may have been one or two lectures on testing, usually by faculty in the discipline who had no specialized training in constructing valid and reliable tests. On many campuses faculty specialists in testing from the psychology department conduct seminars for new faculty on test construction, and indeed many experienced faculty participate in such training.

Grades and grading

The terms grading and marking are used interchangeably and refer to evaluation recorded in some standardized shorthand manner. The grade may be based on some absolute standard in which a stated level of achievement is defined and the grade represents the extent to which the student has achieved it, sometimes called criterion-referenced grading; or it may be 'normative' in that students' performances are compared with one another.

Letter grades A, B, C, D and F are used by 88 per cent of four-year arts and sciences colleges and 99 per cent of four-year professional and technical colleges and only slightly fewer two-year colleges (Levine, 1978). Grade F indicates failure; D is usually acceptable at the undergraduate level but many departments will not accept a D in the major field of study. Undergraduates must earn a C average, that is, balance every D with a B grade, in order to receive a degree.

A very small number of institutions use numerical grades, that is, 1 to 100, but this method is not popular for several reasons, among them the fact that it suggests a degree of measurement precision in assessing student learning that is rarely achieved.

In response to the student revolution in the 1960s many institutions instituted alternative grading patterns or provided options. The most common is pass/fail; another is credit-no credit. In the latter case, if the student passes the course, a mark of CR goes into his records, but if he does not, the course does not usually appear on his permanent records. The primary argument for both P/F and CR/NC grading is to permit students to take courses outside their major fields of study for enrichment for which they lack adequate background. Most colleges and universities permit students to register for some courses on a P/F basis, although there are many variations of its use and the restrictions applied to it. CR/NC is more common at the graduate level.

A small number of institutions use written evaluations, consisting of descriptions of student performance in essay form but many that have tried the system discontinued it because of the time required to prepare the reports properly.

Undergraduate students are usually required to maintain a C average in order to remain in college, although they are permitted to have less than a C average temporarily, for one or two semesters. For computation, numerical values are assigned to grades as follows: A=4; B=3; C=2; D=1; F=0. Thus a requirement of a C average is often listed as a requirement of 2 average, and referred to as grade point average (GPA). For admission most graduate schools require an undergraduate GPA of 3 or B average, if not for all undergraduate study, at least for the last sixty credits.

Among the alternatives tried during the self-examination period colleges and universities experienced in the 1960s and early 1970s were the four descriptors; high pass, pass, low pass, fail; but the end results were so similar to the traditional grading system that most institutions dropped the idea.

Textbooks and other materials

In almost all courses the selection of textbooks and other teaching materials is the prerogrative of the teacher, but there are exceptions. In some large departments that have multiple sections of courses, all the faculty teaching sections of a course may jointly approve the textbook to use. Where some of the sections are taught by teaching assistants, that is, graduate students, the textbooks may be selected by the faculty member supervising the teaching.

Graduate courses frequently require no textbook but instead the teacher distributes to students a bibliography of books and journal articles they are expected to read. Most undergraduate courses require texts and in laboratory courses very often workbooks as well. The typical course requires one or two textbooks but it is not unusual for literature courses to require five to ten books, most of which are usually available in paperback form.

Books and classroom materials are published by private publishing firms. Occasionally a teacher will find a publication of a federal agency useful and require students to buy it from the Government Printing Office. Foundations, trade or professional associations, and quasi-governmental agencies are occasionally sources of books and teaching materials but, with these exceptions, private book publishers are the major source of materials. In recent years some reference books have begun to be replaced by publications in microform, that is, microfilm and microfiche, plus movie film and audio tape. Books that may not be profitable are sometimes published by university presses, although they do not generally specialize in textbooks.

Books, workbooks, laboratory manuals and other materials for which the demand may be limited are often duplicated within a professor's institution and sold by a local bookshop. Such materials are sometimes published later on by a major publisher for national sales.

Neither the federal government nor state governments publish textbooks or other teaching materials as a general practice; however many publications produced by both in connection with other undertakings, such as conferences, commission studies, research, and others, are purchased by college and university libraries and some are used as course references.

Among the many ways publishers promote the sale of their textbooks is to provide a gratis copy to the teacher if the book is adopted for class use and students are required to purchase it.

Almost all the college and university textbooks are written by faculty members. Leading publishers expect their sales people to maintain contact with potential authors. A few faculty have got rich from books written for freshman and sophomore classes where enrolments are large; but for most faculty who write books the returns are small. Publishers pay modest royalties on textbooks, usually from 5 per cent to 15 per cent in the US, averaging 10 to 12 per cent of the wholesale price of the book. Faculty who write books usually do so for the satisfaction it brings rather than income. In some fields of study authorship of a book is a factor, indeed in some cases a requirement for promotion in rank. Authorship also brings visibility to the faculty member, establishes him as an authority on a topic, and can lead to an invitation to appear on programmes at national meetings of his discipline, to address non-university groups for a fee, to consult, or to serve as expert witness before congressional or legislative committees, courtroom trials and investigating committees.

Academic advising

Most colleges and universities divide the task of advising students on academic matters and counselling them on non-academic matters. In most institutions a student is assigned to a faculty member upon admission who works with him to plan a degree programme and select courses within the options available, in addition to those required in his curriculum, to fit the student's interests and career plans.

In some institutions academic advising of undergraduate students is allocated to one or more faculty members in a department who have particular talent for it with adjustments in their workload. In other cases all academic advising is done by an assistant dean and other staff members in the office of the dean of the college or school. This plan is more common in professional schools than in arts and sciences. Many students find this approach too impersonal and prefer advice from a faculty member who often becomes the student's mentor and sometimes a father or mother figure.

Counselling concerning psychological problems and personal matters is the responsibility of professionally trained counsellors located in a counselling centre elsewhere on campus. None the less it is not unusual for students who have developed a trusting relationship with a faculty academic adviser to seek from him or her counsel on a wide variety of personal matters — boy friend or girl friend problems, money problems,

140

relationships with parents, relationships with room-mates and peers, career concerns, and many more. Often problems concerning alcohol, drugs, emotional security, potential suicide and other serious psychological problems are brought first to the academic adviser who will encourage the student to seek professional counselling.

The academic adviser must deal with a student's wish to solve short-term problems while seeing the need for a different solution for his long-term benefit. For example, students often prefer to take easier undergraduate courses in order to earn higher grades and enhance their chances for admission to graduate study or medical, law or other professional schools, while faculty advisers may try to persuade them to take courses, often more difficult, which will help prepare them to benefit most from later studies.

Some students arrive at college with their educational plans firm and make no changes, but about half the undergraduates change their major field of study at least once, and some several times while in college. The reasons vary but usually relate to a lack of information or maturity. Students planning to major in engineering, business administration or some other professional field at the undergraduate level usually declare their majors upon admission to college but those planning to study in the arts and sciences are often not required to decide on a major until the end of their freshman year and in some institutions not until the end of their sophomore year. For the student who goes to college with only a vague notion of what his major might be this provides an opportunity to become acquainted with several fields of study before choosing a major.

Students enrolling in community colleges, except those interested in vocational-technical fields, are not likely to have chosen a major field of study upon admission. Many say that one of their objectives in attending a community college is to determine which fields of study interest them. Since the role of the academic adviser always goes well beyond course selection, many community colleges use full-time academic advisers who have professional training in counselling to advise students academically. Other counsellors are available for students with serious emotional problems, but full-time academic counsellors in community colleges provide the student advice and counsel on problems that few faculty members are prepared to handle. Full-time academic counsellors are also found in a few four-year colleges.

At the graduate level the student most often has an assigned adviser who also serves as mentor. At the doctoral level the student may be the adviser's paid research assistant whose doctoral dissertation research consists of an aspect of a larger study by the faculty adviser. At the master's degree level, which relies more on predetermined curriculum requirements, the student may have minimal contact with an adviser, and in some programmes such as the MBA, where the curriculum is relatively inflexible, the student may have no assigned adviser other than an assistant dean responsible for all MBA students.

Office hours

Faculty members are not in their offices at all times when not in class. In the sciences they spend many hours in laboratories engaged in research. Faculty in the humanities and social sciences are likely to spend more time in the library. Most faculty maintain an office or study at home and work there much of the time in the belief that in preparing lectures, preparing course syllabuses, marking tests and papers, writing research proposals and reports, and other academic duties they can accomplish more than in their office on campus.

To be available to students virtually all faculty post office hours. Some institutions require a minimum of ten office hours per week but in most the number is left to the faculty member's discretion, and may be as few as three or as many as fifteen hours per week.

Student-faculty relationships

The cultural setting of the academic world has changed markedly since the 1950s. In earlier times a professor was regarded with some awe and treated with deference. That began to change during the student revolt of the 1960s as academe moved increasingly towards egalitarianism in student-faculty relationships. During the 1960s students with strong commitment to egalitarianism regarded professors with less awe, accorded them less deference and dealt with them essentially as equals, including addressing them by their first names. Many of those students are now professors and still feel that students and faculty should have a familiar relationship, and some insist on students addressing them by their first names.

Before the 1960s many institutions forbid faculty to date or otherwise have a personal relationship with a student, and while it is still discouraged, the restrictions are now more ambiguous except in more conservative colleges, especially those with religious affiliation.

While published rules concerning student-faculty relationships have declined on each campus, there are unwritten codes of behaviour to guide faculty. These may include prohibition against borrowing money from students or lending money to them, participating in any illegal action with students such as use of drugs, advising students to violate a law, permitting students to commit theft, and so on. What is acceptable in student-faculty relationships differs widely among institutions, for example, what is acceptable in a large city might be unacceptable in a small town and relationships that are acceptable in a large research university might be taboo in a community college or church-related college. Even if institutions were inclined to publish common rules concerning student-faculty relationships it is unlikely that much agreement could be reached among institutions because of the autonomy of institutions and the variability in what is acceptable.

Academic quality

For the development and maintenance of academic quality institutions must rely almost entirely on their faculties. Administrators and boards of trustees can encourage faculty to provide high quality education and seek higher standards but the decision is up to faculty, which makes the selection of faculty so critical to the future of the institution.

There is wide variation in quality among institutions in the US. Research and doctoral universities and selective liberal arts colleges with high percentages of faculty who hold the doctorate and were trained at leading graduate schools are likely to offer the best quality of education. Institutions whose faculty are less well trained and who received their graduate degrees from less distinguished institutions are less likely to provide higher quality education. There are many exceptions but the principle is valid.

The mechanism for assuring the public that an institution offers programmes of acceptable quality is achieved through voluntary accreditation. Both the federal and state governments accept accreditation by a regional accrediting body as evidence of acceptable institutional quality.

Regional accreditation

There are six regional accrediting associations in the US; each state is located in a region served by one of these associations. An institution is eligible for membership (accreditation) only in the association in the region in which it is located. Each regional accrediting association accredits elementary and secondary schools, vocational-technical schools, and colleges and universities and has separate staffs for each group.

The six regional accrediting associations are voluntary autonomous organizations, each with a separate division for higher education whose rules and regulations are determined by representatives of member colleges and universities. Neither the federal government nor any state government has control over the deliberations and actions of the accrediting bodies.

143

A college or university that wishes to become accredited makes application to the accrediting association in its region, which sets in motion a lengthy process. Each association has an executive staff which spends much of its time managing accreditation visits to institutions. Well established institutions with programmes of acceptable quality are inspected every ten years. Institutions applying for accreditation for the first time, such as new institutions, and those with deficiencies receive a second visit within five years, sometimes sooner.

The inspection team is composed of ten to twenty-five members, selected by the higher education staff of the association from member institutions, depending on the size and complexity of the institution to be visited.

The visit is preceded by a self-study of the institution lasting from twelve to eighteen months at the end of which a comprehensive report is prepared and sent to the team beforehand. During the visit, which usually lasts four or five days, the team members seek clarification of portions of the report and evidence of statements and also make detailed investigations of their own. Among matters examined are: qualifications of faculty, admission requirements and conditions for retention and dismissal, the institution's physical plant and other facilities and equipment, its financial health, size and quality of library holdings, teaching procedures, academic requirements, faculty workload, classroom, laboratory and other teaching and research space, student services and programmes, plus others.

Following the visit the team reports to the governing board of the association which decides whether the institution is qualified for membership, that is, accreditation. If the board approves, then its recommendation goes to the delegate assembly of representatives of member institutions, which meets annually. Only a small number of institutions fail to gain accreditation through this process; more commonly an institution which has deficiencies will be informed and given a period to correct the deficiencies before a final decision is made.

While accreditation by its regional accrediting association is not required for an institution to operate, it is highly desirable. Failure to achieve accreditation by the regional accrediting association has several disadvantages: it may disqualify students who apply for federal or state financial aid; disqualify the institution for federal grants and contracts; it may prevent its graduates from earning licences to practice a profession; and graduates who transfer to accredited institutions may find their credits from a non-accredited institution unacceptable for transfer.

144

Professional accreditation

In addition to regional accreditation there are approximately sixty associations that accredit specific programmes, for example, chemistry, music, teacher education, business administration, law, medicine, pharmacy, dentistry, and so on. Lack of accreditation may be only a minor drawback but for individual students it can be a major handicap: some graduate and professional schools will only accept students who have completed accredited undergraduate degree programmes. In the case of licensing for medical practice, dentistry and other professions some states will only licence persons who have completed degrees in accredited schools.

The number of professional accrediting associations has grown so rapidly in recent years that an organization known as the Council on Postsecondary Education was formed to coordinate accrediting activities and set standards for accrediting associations.

A professional accrediting team proceeds in a manner similar to that described for regional accreditation but limits its examination to one field, and because it is examining only one field of study it is more thorough.

Federal and state roles

The federal government has to date refrained from engaging in accreditation, although the matter has been discussed from time to time in connection with legislation to provide funds for accredited institutions. In each case the Congress has decided that the various agencies of the government should rely on the results of voluntary accreditation.

Many states require periodic inspection of teacher education programmes by their state departments of education; the procedure is much the same as a visit by a regional accreditation team. In some states appropriate state agencies visit and inspect institutions for accreditation in other fields of study, and indeed in a few states, for example, New York, a state agency conducts an accreditation visit of each public and private college and university in its state. But most states accept the judgment of the regional accrediting association so that if an institution meets that association's standards, it is automatically approved by the state.

Libraries

Next to faculty the most important ingredient of an institution of quality is a good library. Regional accrediting teams place high value on the size and quality of an institution's library; accrediting teams of professional associations are also concerned with the quantity and quality of library holdings in the field under investigation, particularly if the institution offers graduate degrees in that field.

One measure of the quality of an institution is the portion of its budget spent on purchase of books and other materials and services. All the leading research and doctoral degree granting universities have library collections in excess of 1 million volumes; Harvard leads with more than 10 million volumes.

In addition to their own collection almost all libraries participate in a lending programme through which they can borrow library materials they do not possess from other colleges and universities. Much library material is now available on microfilm and microfiche, which takes less storage space and is often the only source of back numbers of newspapers, scholarly journals and other periodicals.

Cataloguing, once a slow, costly and tedious task, is now faster, more accurate and less costly through two national computer-based cataloguing systems. Most colleges and universities use one of these services which catalogue all new publications and store the data in their computers. Libraries can contact their computers by telephone and receive data electronically for cataloguing books and other publications.

Until recent years many institutions used the Dewey decimal system for cataloguing but most have instituted the Library of Congress cataloguing system, which is used by the national cataloguing centres. The Library of Congress in Washington, DC receives copies of all materials that are copyrighted and many that are not.

Thanks to computers many libraries provide services not heard of a decade or so ago. They have replaced handwritten pieces of paper previously required to borrow books from a library with a system whereby a computer reads a bar code on the book and on the identification card of the borrower and stores both in the computer.

The development of bibliographies, once a slow process, is now possible by computer. In some fields the bibliographical contents of all issues of professional journals are filed in a computer by an organization established for that purpose. When a student or faculty member wants a bibliography on a problem area or other aspect of his field, the college or university library can obtain a computer print-out for him from the national centre computer via the telephone.

Because of the computer the modern library has much better control of its collections than heretofore and can perform many of its functions more accurately and at much less cost than by hand.

Unlike older universities in some European cities where institutes and faculties are dispersed throughout the city, almost all American colleges and universities are located on a single campus, unless the institution has branch campuses. As a consequence each institution is normally served by a single library, although in many large universities there may be a library for undergraduates in addition to the main library which is intended to support research.

Decentralized or branch libraries were more common thirty or forty years ago; the engineering collection would be located in the building housing engineering, education would be located in the education building, and so on. This is still true for medicine and law, and in many large universities some professional schools and departments maintain a small collection in their building, but this is declining. The coming of technology in libraries made the cost of providing many services to branch libraries prohibitive. Although faculty and students are more likely to make maximum use of a branch library located in or near the building where they have classes, efficiency and the variety and quality of services argue for centralization of libraries on a campus.

Academic ceremonies

Most institutions hold commencement ceremonies only once a year in May or June, at the end of the academic year. Students who complete degree requirements at the end of the summer term or the end of the first semester are officially awarded a diploma at the one commencement, along with May or June graduates. But in other institutions, especially very large universities, commencement is held at the end of the summer session, and each semester or quarter.

Students and faculty wear traditional academic robes and march in procession to music played by the student marching band, usually to 'Pomp and Circumstance'. A commencement programme begins with a welcome and introduction of platform guests by the president of the institution, followed by an address by a distinguished personage, often a political figure, scientist or person of letters. Honorary degrees, if any, are then awarded. Finally degrees are awarded to graduates. In a small college all students pass individually across the stage to receive their diplomas from the university president or dean. Before this ceremony however the degrees are officially conferred on the graduates as a group, usually by the president, but occasionally by the chairman of the board of trustees. In a small institution graduates are asked to rise according to the degree they are to receive, that is, BS, BA, BBA, and so on, and the president or chairman intones the words they have waited to hear for four years.

In large universities which may have 3000 or 4000 graduates it is impracticable for each student to walk across the stage and receive a diploma. Instead degrees are awarded by the college or school, the dean of which certifies ceremonially that the students qualify for their degrees and the president bestows them. Diplomas are collected afterwards from a central distribution point or posted to graduates. In such cases the only degree recipients to cross the stage are graduates of academic doctoral degrees, that is, the PhD, EdD, DMA, and so on, at which time each recipient has a hood in the colours of the university and his field of study placed on him by the president or dean of the graduate school. Recipients of MD, DDS and JD degrees are not usually hooded in the ceremony.

Some large universities continue to present diplomas to all graduates and do it by having six, eight or ten lines moving forward at one time, with the deans of the respective schools and colleges handing out diplomas and congratulating graduates. When large numbers of students are presented diplomas a so-called dummy diploma rolled and tied with a ribbon is given the graduate to avoid issuing the actual diploma to the wrong person, since at the last minute one or more graduates often fail to appear.

Convocation

Most colleges and universities have one, sometimes two convocation ceremonies annually. The most common is in the spring. In many institutions faculty, but not students, appear in academic costume. The programme highlight is a scholarly paper by the president or some other officer, a member of the faculty or a guest speaker who may be from another university or from outside academe. In many cases the occasion is known as honours convocation at which time students who have earned various academic awards and recognition receive them amid appropriate ceremony.

In small colleges assemblies occur more frequently and create a sense of community not possible in a university of 20 000 or more students. During the 1960s some students and faculty developed an aversion to ceremony and on some campuses few faculty attended commencement or convocation. During the 1970s faculty returned to ceremony wearing academic regalia, but at many large institutions only a small percentage of faculty still choose to participate in commencement, not in protest but through lack of interest.

Concern about teaching, whether faculty devote enough time to it, whether it is of adequate quality and other questions related to the learning process are continually under discussion on almost every campus in America. The extent of this concern and the kinds and amount of activities conducted to influence the improvement of teaching fluctuate but never disappear. In the mid-1980s the major concern was inadequate preparation of college students in elementary and secondary schools, a consequence of which was that almost all American institutions of higher learning, including some of the most prestigious, were required to offer subcollegiate instruction to remedy inadequate secondary school preparation, particularly in writing and mathematics.

Although many critics of American higher education complain that faculty give inadequate attention to teaching, the dedication with which most faculty approach the teaching task largely belies this charge.

7 Students

Anyone reading about college students of the late 1960s would be struck by the attention given to the generation gap. Students, particularly the radicals, talked a great deal about it and at radical rallies 'don't trust anyone over thirty' was heard over and over again.

By the 1980s little was heard of this. The radicals themselves were past thirty and the new college students were not interested in protest. With the fear of nuclear war, the growing shortage of preferred jobs and other matters that concern students, their interests changed and they became much more concerned about their own future.

Students became more conservative. A survey of 192 435 entering freshmen at 365 colleges and universities in 1985 found that most students considered themselves middle of the road politically while the remainder were equally divided between liberal and conservative (CHE, 15 January 1986). Some observers of higher education found student attitudes and behaviours in the 1980s similar to those of the 1950s with respect to activism: disinterest in public issues and concern for their own education and future.

In some respects however students of the 1970s and 1980s were like those of the 1960s. Despite the fact that a high percentage relied on some form of student financial aid, they were products of the affluent society, accustomed to enjoying the comforts of adult life and not imbued with need for thrift. While most students in the 1950s lived in dormitories or low-cost off-campus housing, students twenty-five or thirty years later rented comfortable apartments off campus, owned cars and routinely attended entertainment events that students of an earlier period would have considered beyond their means. To be sure many students had barely enough income to finance educational expenses, yet a large percentage managed to enjoy 'the good life' while attending college.

Pre-collegiate education

Twelve years of free public elementary and secondary education are provided in each state. Compulsory school attendance begins at the age of six or seven and continues to age sixteen. In most states public schools provide free kindergarten schooling for five-year-old children. Pre-school education is not provided by many public school systems; however nursery schools are available in most communities on a fee basis. Many are operated by churches, some by industries and businesses for their employees, others by cooperative associations of parents and the largest number as private enterprises, some of them by women in their homes.

In the first six years of school all pupils are in the same class, receive instruction in the same subjects and by a single teacher in each grade. In some schools, elementary (primary) school extends to the eighth grade and secondary school, also called high school, consists of grades nine to twelve. This pattern is more often found in small communities. In larger communities other patterns are found. The leading model consists of six years of elementary education after which pupils transfer to a junior high school for grades seven to nine and then transfer to a senior high school for grades ten to twelve. A second model involves transfer after five years at an elementary school to a middle school for grades six to nine, then to a senior high school for grades ten to twelve.

Beginning in the junior high school or middle school, students have some choice of curriculum, and in senior high school there is greater choice. Generally there are three lines or tracks in the senior high school, although most schools do not label them to avoid any stigma that might accrue to one track. The academic track is for students who are preparing to enter college and includes more required courses in English, history, science and mathematics, and often includes a foreign language. The vocational curriculum is designed for pupils who plan to join the workforce immediately upon leaving school and consists of as much as half time on vocational subjects, often including part-time work experience in fields such as retailing, electronics repair, food preparation, automotive mechanics, secretarial work and others. The general curriculum is designed for pupils whose post-secondary plans are not determined and who seek a general education. It is less demanding than the academic curriculum, yet many of those enrolled later decide to attend college and do so without additional preparation. In the early 1980s, 38 per cent of the high school seniors were enrolled in the academic curriculum, 24 per cent in the vocational curriculum and 36 per cent in the general curriculum. The three lines are usually not so designated officially and often can be discerned only by examination of the courses students choose. During the first two years of high school most of the students take the same courses — English, history, science, mathematics and other basic subjects. As they near completion of high school they choose courses that are identified with the academic, vocational or general curriculum.

Early in the twentieth century many school systems awarded students diplomas upon completion of the secondary school indicating which curriculum each had completed but many educators and citizens felt that this carried social connotations that were inappropriate for a democracy. There is some indication however that some educators and many citizens are beginning to consider reinstituting this or a similar plan.

The foregoing description of public elementary and secondary education presents only the sketchiest overview; within this framework are many variations. Some public schools, located in high income communities with pupils from homes of educated parents, are characterized by high levels of academic achievement, high percentages of their graduates attend college and the schools constitute no serious social problem. At the other end of the spectrum are the inner city schools which are attended largely by black or Hispanic children from low income families, many of whom have limited exposure to an intellectual environment in the home and whose out-of-school experiences do not contribute to a positive attitude towards schooling. These schools experience disruption, less learning and frustration for teachers and pupils. Despite many efforts by state and federal governments to improve the schooling of inner city youth, progress is slow due in large measure not only to economic disadvantages but cultural deprivation in the home.

There are approximately 85 000 public schools enrolling some 39 million pupils in the US; in addition about 28 000 private schools enrol approximately 6 million pupils or 13 per cent of the elementary and secondary pupils. More than three-quarters of the private schools are sponsored by churches or affiliated with religious groups; almost half the private schools are operated by the Catholic church and account for slightly more than half the pupils enrolled in private elementary and secondary schools.

The Catholic church has a long tradition of operating private schools and historically most of the teachers have been members of Catholic religious orders. The number of private schools operated by Protestant church denominations has increased in recent years due to several factors, including a feeling among many parents that their children were deprived of a desired religious environment in public schools and a belief by some that the quality of education in public schools declined as the numbers of economically and culturally deprived youth in some schools grew, in response to court-ordered integration.

Admission to college

The wide diversity in American higher education is reflected in its admission policies. At one end are a few highly selective colleges that admit only the most highly qualified students; at the other end most community colleges practise open admission which means that they accept any high school graduate or, if not a high school graduate, accept them if they are beyond normal high school age.

Virtually all senior colleges and universities require beginning students to have taken one of the two externally administered admission examinations, *SAT* or *ACT* (see p. 137).

Public institutions

In most states criteria for admission to state colleges and universities are set by the faculty, administration and boards of trustees but with the knowledge that state legislatures may protest if institutions become too selective. In some parts of the country, particularly the South, state legislatures tend to feel that all high school graduates should be eligible to enrol in a state college or university. In other parts of the country legislatures are more tolerant of selectivity. For example, in the state of California the leading state universities admit only the most academically talented secondary school graduates, but the nineteen colleges and universities in the California State University system are less selective, admitting most students who rank in the top half of their secondary school graduating classes. The community colleges accept any secondary school graduate, and in certain circumstances non-graduates as well. After a period of study at a state college or community college, if the student's academic record so merits, he may transfer to a university to which he was ineligible for admission based on his secondary school academic performance.

Approximately thirty public universities exercise a high degree of selectivity; among them are the University of California at Berkeley, University of Michigan, University of Virginia, College of William and Mary (in Virginia), University of North Carolina at Chapel Hill, Miami University (in Ohio) and the University of California at San Diego.

In addition to another twenty or so highly selective public institutions, many state colleges and universities limit enrolment in selected disciplines for which the number of applications is greater than the institution can accommodate. This is often true for admission to undergraduate study in engineering, architecture, pharmacy, and sometimes business administration.

Regional state colleges and universities usually require only graduation from a secondary school for admission but in the mid-1980s, in response to widespread belief that too many students were arriving at college inadequately prepared, some public colleges and universities began to require specific secondary school courses for admission. In several states the state board for elementary and secondary education required more academic subjects for a high school diploma, which had the effect of improving the preparation of students enrolling in higher education. For many students who would earlier have taken the general curriculum this change required them in effect to complete a college preparatory curriculum.

Community colleges, most of which receive all or part of their funding from local taxes and which emphasize meeting the needs of the communities in which they are located, make special effort to accommodate the disadvantaged, the student whose academic background is less than laudable, and young people who are trying to decide what to do with their lives, in addition to more able students who have firm career plans and are fully capable of doing college level work. While many of the less academically qualified students choose vocational-technical curricula in the community college, some choose academic or general curricula with a view to transferring to a senior college or university. Although the majority do not transfer but instead enter the work force after two years or less at a community college, most tax-payers seem to agree that tax funds spent to provide these young people with some post-secondary education is a good investment for society.

Both community colleges and non-selective state colleges and universities stress the value of giving students a chance to succeed in college even though their qualifications for college level work may be marginal or deficient. As previously noted, in some state universities as many as a quarter do not return for the second year, either from choice or because of their lack of academic preparation and failure.

Failure is less common in community colleges, for several reasons. Most community colleges employ counsellors and some allocate faculty time to tutorials to help students who are deficient to improve their performance. And although there are many community colleges with demanding academic standards, community college courses are not generally as demanding academically and a student can maintain a passing grade with lower performance than in state universities. In addition most community colleges permit students whose academic performance is not satisfactory to continue longer than do most state colleges and universities. Community college faculty and administrators stress that this is a part of their policy of giving young people every possible chance to succeed.

Private institutions

The most selective colleges and universities are found in the private sector. Among the most selective private institutions are Harvard, Stanford, Chicago, Brown, Princeton, Rice and Yale universities, Amherst, Reed, Swarthmore, Williams, Pomona and Dartmouth colleges, and Massachusetts Institute of Technology and California Institute of Technology. For example, Harvard, Yale, Princeton and Stanford universities admit between 17 and 20 per cent of the applicants to undergraduate study.

Just over a hundred private liberal arts colleges can be considered highly selective; however of the approximately 1000 private colleges that offer liberal arts studies about half practise some degree of selectivity. All the remainder require graduation from a secondary school, some require specific courses in secondary school preparation and, although all entrants will have taken the SAT or ACT exam, the scores acceptable for admission are low enough to accommodate most applicants. Many of these colleges are church-related and students choose them because of the religious environment; some accept only women students, a few serve a limited geographic area and some persist through intensive student recruitment.

Admission procedures

Students who wish to attend a selective college or university usually take the SAT or ACT admission exam not later than the summer before their final year of secondary school, often earlier, and before Christmas submit an application to one or more institutions they wish to attend. The more selective colleges and universities receive between five and ten applications for each student admitted, and students often apply to several institutions to ensure admission to one of their choice.

In most of the selective institutions the director of admissions organizes applications and, with the assistance of an admissions committee, which may be composed of faculty, students and admissions staff, selects those to be admitted, based on criteria established for the institution. By common agreement these institutions notify applicants by 1 April and, if accepted, request them to confirm acceptance by 1 May, usually with a tuition deposit, although as the numbers of applicants decline the 1 May deadline is becoming increasingly flexible in all but the most selective institutions. In addition to the applicants accepted, a 'wait' list is informed that if any of the first list does not accept the admission offer, they may be offered admission later.

There is no central applications centre or process as in the Federal Republic of Germany, Great Britain and some other countries and because of the diversity of public and private institutions it is unlikely that such a system would succeed in the US. It could succeed among public institutions in a given state, but since few state colleges and universities are highly selective there is no need for it. Each initial application costs $15 to $75, so even if the individual accepts only one offer but applies to several institutions a considerable amount of money may be involved.

In non-selective colleges and universities students are at liberty to apply later and the admission process is normally handled by a staff member who examines applications to see that technical requirements, such as grade point average and SAT score, are acceptable and informs the student of acceptance.

Finally community colleges usually require only that the student show evidence of secondary school completion; they usually request advanced application but a substantial percentage of new community college students appear for registration without having made application in advance. Normally all are accepted. Admission of students who transfer from one college or university to another is based to a considerable extent on grades at the previous institution, rather than secondary school achievement. Score on the SAT or ACT exam is important if the transfer student has completed less than a full year of college study when entering. In many institutions the academic standards of the institution from which the student transfers are considered in determining admission. Although most students spend all four undergraduate years at the same institution, a considerable number attend two or more institutions before completing a degree; it is not unusual for an older student receiving a baccalaureate degree to have attended three or four colleges and/or universities.

Approximately 85 per cent of students enrolled in colleges and universities are residents of the state in which the institution is located. This percentage is higher for undergraduates and lower for graduate students. Among private institutions the percentage is much lower because most of them do not consider the state in which they are located as the sole source of students. Many of the leading private institutions strive to achieve an enrolment composed of students from many different states. All state institutions charge additional fees for out of state students but private institutions do not.

Admission to graduate study and to postgraduate professional schools is on a selective basis in almost all cases. Admission to graduate study usually requires the student to have a B average in the last two years of undergraduate study and a satisfactory score on the Graduate Record Examination, which varies among institutions and fields of study. Some institutions and departments also require letters of recommendation and other evidence of likelihood of success in graduate study.

Students applying for admission to a medical school must have a high grade point average at the undergraduate level, a high score on the Medical College Admission Test (MCAT) and satisfy other criteria that differ among institutions. On average medical schools receive two to three applications for each student admitted; however because students know how demanding medical schools are, only those with high grades and MCAT scores apply.

The better law schools are selective, requiring not only high undergraduate grades and a high score on the Law School Admission Test but other evidence of likelihood of success. However a few law schools are relatively non-selective, requiring only a bachelor's degree with a modest grade point average for admission; some of these are not associated with a university and offer evening programmes only.

Enrolment

College attendance escalated rapidly after the Second World War. In 1929—30 it totalled 1.1 million; by 1960 it totalled 3.6 million, an increase of 227 per cent in thirty years, but the fastest growth occurred between 1960 and 1970. Enrolment in 1970 was 8.65 million, an increase of 140 per cent in ten years and in 1980 it was approximately 12.1 million, an increase of 236 per cent in twenty years.

By 1979 three-quarters of the appropriate age group were graduating from secondary school and of that number 59 per cent enrolled in college. Just a few years ago 50 per cent of those who enrolled in college failed to complete a baccalaureate degree but by 1980 that had dropped to 40 per cent and continues to decline gradually. During the same time, however, patterns of college attendance changed. No longer do all students continue uninterruptedly for four years; stopping out has become common. As stated before, in community colleges and some urban commuter colleges as many as a quarter of the students may not return every semester. They interrupt their studies to earn money, to pursue full-time employment, to move to another city, to assume family responsibilities and for many other reasons.

Demographers had predicted large declines in college attendance due to a sharp drop in births in the 1960s and 1970s, particularly in the north-eastern part of the country, but the college attendance rate did not decline proportionately to the decline in eighteen-year-old youth. Several factors contributed to this. There was an increase in the number of women, blacks and Hispanics attending college; more older people returned to college; there was a considerable increase in part-time attendance; a sharp increase in community college enrolments due, in part, to broadening the curriculum offerings that attracted students who would not have attended college earlier; more specialized institutions and programmes catering to new student interests; and upgrading of requirements in some professions requiring further professional or graduate study.

The increase of older students and less affluent students, many of whom work part-time or full-time, is due in part to the many public community colleges and senior colleges and universities opened during the 1960s and early 1970s in cities where low cost public higher education had not previously been available. This provided higher education opportunities not only for new college students but made it possible for employed people to pursue graduate degrees. In some public urban universities enrolment of graduate students almost equals the number of juniors and seniors enrolled and as many as 75 per cent are part-time students.

Part-time study

Among the private, more prestigious universities and liberal arts colleges there are few part-time students. Many do not admit them and others discourage them by charging the same tuition for part-time as full-time students.

Following the Second World War and the move towards mass higher education in the United States, both community colleges and senior colleges and universities were established in larger population centres and cater for part-time enrolment. The older premier public universities admit part-time students who account for relatively small portions of their enrolments — less than 8 per cent at the University of California at Berkeley and less than 10 per cent at the University of Illinois at Urbana.

At the newer urban universities the percentages of part-time students are higher, for example, the main campuses of the University of South Florida in Tampa, 45 per cent, and the University of Houston, 46 per cent.

In most community colleges the majority of students enrol for part-time study. According to the US Department of Education, in the early 1980s part-time students accounted for 59 per cent of the enrolment at Miami-Dade Community College in Florida, 70 per cent at Cuyahoga Community College in Cleveland, Ohio, and 89 per cent at Long Beach City College in California.

158

Profiles of students

The first women's colleges were founded in the 1830s. College attendance rose rapidly during the latter part of the nineteenth century. As recently as 1960 women accounted for just over one-third of those enrolled in colleges and universities but by 1982 women were in the majority. They constituted more than 50 per cent at the undergraduate level and almost half at the graduate level. Among students over thirty-five, two-thirds were women. By 1980 women constituted 26 per cent of the beginning students in medical schools, 34 per cent in law schools and 45 per cent in business schools.

Beginning with the Civil Rights Act of 1964 and with subsequent legislation, large amounts of money and effort were dedicated to increasing minority enrolments in colleges and universities, principally blacks and Hispanics, since Asian-Americans had for many years been enrolling in colleges in greater numbers than their percentage in society. By 1980 the proportion of black high school graduates attending college equalled that of whites.

There are major differences in student characteristics according to the type of institution. Students who attend public colleges and universities in New York City, for example, differ markedly from the national student population. The City University of New York consists of eighteen colleges and universities, including seven community colleges, all urban, serving commuter students. In the early 1980s they enrolled 178 000 students of whom 56 per cent were women who constituted 63 per cent of enrolment in community colleges and 69 per cent of the graduate enrolment. Approximately 55 per cent were black, Hispanic, Asian or members of other minority groups, of which 30 per cent came from homes where English was not the first language. About 30 per cent were employed full-time; 57 per cent of the senior college and university students and 44 per cent of the community college students worked full-time or part-time. The average undergraduate student was twenty-six years old and only about half entered a college or university directly from high school; the average age of entering freshmen in community colleges was twenty-two and in senior colleges and universities twenty. Approximately one-third of the community college students and 22 per cent of the senior college and university students came from homes with family incomes of less than $8000 (the federal government then considered $9860 the poverty line for a family of four). Almost 75 per cent of the full-time undergraduate students received some kind of financial aid from federal, state or city government, the institution and other sources.

The profile of students at the City University of New York is in sharp contrast in many ways to students at other types of institution;

this plus the location of the institutions and other factors results in a far different kind of educational and social experience compared with other institutions.

A more typical profile of all American undergraduate students can be inferred from the sample (see p. 150) of 192 435 freshmen students at 365 colleges and universities of all types surveyed in 1985 (*CHE*, 15 January 1986). Of the total, 93 per cent had gone straight from secondary school to college and 95 per cent were nineteen years of age or less. The college they were attending was not the first choice for about a quarter of the students although financial limitations more than failure to be admitted was more often the reason. Some 66 per cent had applied for admission to two or more institutions and of these 82 per cent had been accepted by two or more. About 71 per cent came from homes where the mother worked outside the home, either full-time or part-time. One out of five attended college within ten miles of their parents' homes, and 54.2 per cent attended a college or university more than fifty miles from their parents' homes.

Their planned fields of study were: engineering 10.7 per cent; education 6.2 per cent; business 23.9 per cent; physical and biological sciences 5.8 per cent; social and behavioural sciences 8.6 per cent; arts and humanities 6.2 per cent, with the remainder distributed among many fields.

Paying for college

Historically students attending college relied on family savings. Beginning at birth middle-class families created savings funds to pay for children's college expenses. This is still true for many middle-class families, particularly if they aspire for their children to attend expensive private colleges or universities.

Beginning in the 1960s major changes have occurred in the way students pay college expenses. The national government had earlier provided grants to war veterans so that they could attend college and in 1958 loans were made available to students in selected fields of study, but except for the National Youth Administration programme of the 1930s, which was primarily in response to the national economic depression, no general financial aid for college students had been provided by the federal government.

Beginning in 1965 several federal programmes were established to provide grants and loans and to subsidize interest on loans for students from low income families. These programmes, established primarily to make it possible for blacks to gain equal access to higher education, were made available to all students from low income families and made it possible for everyone to attend college. In addition to programmes based on financial need the federal government provides funds for college attendance to children of deceased military servicemen, for handicapped students and several other categories of persons.

Following the creation of federal programmes to assist students from low income families, most state governments established various student scholarship, grant and loan programmes to supplement federal funds. Most state financial aid is in the form of loan funds; they are financed with the sale of tax-exempt bonds and therefore bear a low interest rate. All federal and most state financial aid is available equally to students who attend public and private colleges and universities.

Before 1978 students from families whose income was above the poverty level had less access to federal financial aid. In that year the Congress passed legislation providing for loans to students whose family income was more than $25 000 per year; termed the Middle Income Student Assistance Act, those loans bear interest well below the market rate and repayment is not required until the student graduates.

Federal and state financial aid programmes do not cover all costs of attending private colleges and universities. Students who wish to attend expensive private institutions must supplement government aid from other sources. Most private institutions, especially the more affluent, are able to provide scholarships, so they can attract blacks, Hispanics and other minority students from low income families and thus have a more balanced student body.

The extent of student reliance on federal and state financial aid programmes is reflected in the 1985 survey of the freshman class, 30 per cent of whom said they received no parental support and another 12 per cent received less than $500 each from parents. Approximately 20 per cent received Pell Grants, that is, basic federal grants to students from low income families, and almost a quarter of that group received supplementary grants because they were from very low income families; 10 per cent participated in the federally funded work-study programme in which students were provided part-time jobs, usually at the college they attended, with 80 per cent of the costs paid by the federal government and 20 per cent by the employer. About 23 per cent of the entering freshmen had loans from private lenders with interest subsidized and repayment guaranteed by the federal government. About 14 per cent received state scholarships or grants and 18 per cent received scholarships or grants from the college they attended. Almost half depended on savings from summer employment to pay part of their expenses.

A survey of the US Department of Labor in 1985 found that 92 per cent of the part-time students and half the full-time students were employed, either full-time or part-time. However that survey was limited to students under twenty-five years of age; it is likely that the percentage of full-time students who held part-time or full-time jobs was higher, since older students are more likely to be employed.

Tuition and fees

Some private colleges include all fees in a single charge, but most institutions levy a tuition fee plus several other fees for various services and purposes, some mandatory and some elective.

According to the College Board tuition and required fees charged by public senior colleges and universities for the 1986–7 academic year (two semesters) averaged $1337 and at private institutions $5793, but averages can be misleading. For example, in one state university in the state of Oklahoma the figure was $540 per year but at a state university in Vermont the total was $3208. Students from outside those states paid an additional $592 and $5270 respectively. At private colleges and universities the range was greater. At one low cost private liberal arts college in the state of Mississippi tuition and fees cost $2384 per year but at a prestigious liberal arts college in the state of New York the annual charge was $11 348. Private universities charge the same for in-state and out of state students. At the more expensive liberal arts colleges tuition and fees, food, housing, books and other expenses pushed the total over $12 000 per year, and in several leading institutions to more than $16 000 per year (*CHE*, 6 August 1986).

Tuition charges in public institutions are greater for out of state students because state taxes are used to pay the cost of operating the institutions. The additional charge is intended to equal the actual cost of educating out of state students but is, in fact, usually far below actual costs. Some adjacent states practise reciprocity in which students from each state can attend public colleges and universities in the other state and pay in-state tuition. In addition graduate teaching and research assistants and others employed half-time or more in the institution they are attending pay in-state tutition.

Following are typical fees a student would pay in a private university: application for admission $25 non-refundable; intent to register $100 non-refundable; tuition $180 per credit or approximately $2700 per semester; advance registration fee $100; housing $925 per semester; meals $600 per semester; student government fee $7; security and breakage deposit $100 refundable; transcript fee $3; student health service $65; and student activities fee (sports, cultural and entertainment events) $30. In addition are several charges that not all students are required to pay: late registration $20; change of class schedule $20; car parking $54; special examination $20; removal of incomplete grade $10; microfilming thesis $15; duplicate identification card $3;

books and supplies approximately $250 per semester; and personal expenses approximately $250 per semester. In addition fees are charged for laboratory courses, for music and art courses involving individual instruction, for ROTC uniforms, for athletics activities courses, for geology field courses, and other special fees depending on a student's curriculum.

Residential arrangements and food service

The extent to which students are immersed in the life of a college or university varies greatly. At one end is the private liberal arts college located in a small town where students live on campus and get not only food and housing but spend most of their free time there, where entertainment and recreation are amply provided. At the other extreme is the commuter student who works full-time and comes to campus only for classes and to use the library; he uses few of the campus facilities and services not related to academic work.

Housing

The typical residential college or university provides dormitories for undergraduate students which may be a private room or involve sharing a room with another student. Many dormitories consist of suites of two bedrooms separated by a living room and bathroom and occasionally a small kitchenette where students can prepare snacks.

Most colleges and universities provide housing on campus — dormitories for single students and small apartments for married students. The exceptions are urban colleges and universities that serve largely, if not solely, local commuter students and community colleges, few of which provide on-campus housing. Almost all private institutions provide campus housing except a few urban institutions and most of them provide a small amount for single students.

Except for undergraduate private liberal arts colleges, most institutions provide on-campus housing for only part of their students. It is not uncommon for a large state university to provide on-campus housing for only a quarter to one-third of the student body.

Since the Second World War most universities and many colleges have provided apartments for married students, either on or near the campus, but these usually accommodate only a portion of the need. The main reason for undersupply of campus housing is that rental payments from students constitute the sole source of income to pay mortgage costs and institutions want to avoid having vacant housing for which there is no income to make payments.

Most campus dormitories are small, housing 200 to 300 students;

this permits most of the students to get to know one another, develop friendships and in other ways enrich the quality of their college experience. One university constructed a dormitory with fourteen floors but found that such a large number of residents contributed to poor relationships among students, aside from the height which some students disliked.

Before the 1970s most residential colleges and universities required undergraduate students to live in dormitories, if not for the entire four years, at least for one or two years. The student protests of the late 1960s involved, among other things, discontent with the degree of supervision and control exercised over their lives by college officials; they protested against the regulations and where possible thousands moved out of campus dormitories to off-campus housing. In some cases colleges had constructed large numbers of dormitories and had regular mortgage payments to be met; when students moved off campus, some dormitories were vacant, which created financial problems.

By the late 1970s rules on behaviour at most institutions were relaxed. This, plus the fact that housing off campus became much more expensive than on campus, caused students to return to dormitory living.

In many institutions regulations that forbade students to be out of their dormitories after 11 or 12 p.m. were abandoned. Selected dorms are co-ed, usually with males and females on alternate floors but in some cases on the same floors at opposite ends of the building. Earlier rules forbidding male and female students to visit one another's rooms have also been relaxed considerably.

Colleges and universities strive to make dormitory living an adjunct to the educational experience. Student residents are organized for sports and social life and share many activities. A staff resident, often a graduate student in psychology or counselling, lives in each dormitory to counsel students and help them to solve both academic and personal problems.

Some colleges still require students to live in college housing, in some cases because they consider it an essential part of the educational experience, and in others, such as colleges with strong religious affiliation, for reasons related to character and morals.

Food service

The cafeteria is standard on all American college and university campuses. Frequently the charge for lodging per semester or academic year includes food service as well. The cafeteria may be located in the student's dormitory or more likely in a separate building to serve students from several dormitories. At very large institutions there will be several cafeterias — one or more serving residential students, one serving commuters, and one or more in the student union. Where several cafeterias exist one of them is likely to provide a variety of foods, for example, Chinese, Mexican, German, Italian, and more.

Many institutions own and operate their own food services but contract food service with a caterer is growing in popularity. Since the mid-1960s hundreds of institutions have switched food service to caterers who assume responsibility for providing food service for all students on campus at a negotiated price per day or per meal, in some cases at weekly or monthly rates. The caterers employ professionals to manage food services and generally students and institutional officials have been pleased with this approach.

For decades students have complained about the quality of food at college and university dining halls. When the food service is handled by institutional employees it is usually difficult if not impossible to replace employees responsible for poor food. When contracting with a caterer a panel of students advises him on student wishes; and since a catering contract can usually be terminated with a few months' notice, caterers strive to satisfy students' desires. Institutions find catering services desirable for several reasons; for example, they are relieved of student complaints about food and they are free of the task of dealing with food service employees, unions and other personnel problems. Many institutions have found that professional catering services can provide quality food at lower cost than institutional food services.

At some institutions many students leave the campus late on Friday until Sunday evening or Monday morning, usually returning to their homes for the weekend. Food services adapt to various student wishes by having cafeteria plans for five days or seven days and a variety of other plans.

Other student services

As noted earlier students are provided with several services for which mandatory fees are charged plus others that are optional. Four of the main ones provided from mandatory fees are the student union, health services, placement and counselling.

Student union

This is the campus centre for social activities. It often contains a cafeteria, snack bars and perhaps a full service restaurant, meeting rooms for clubs and organizations, a ballroom for dances, bowling lanes, cards room, billiard room, bookshop and student supply store, reading rooms, lounges, student government offices, printing and copy service, campus mail centre or post office, and on a few campuses a bar that usually serves only beer and wine.

Health service

Almost all institutions have a student health centre to care for illness and to treat short-term health problems; it is usually staffed by a physician, several in a large institution, plus nurses and other health service personnel and usually has a small clinic where students may be hospitalized for brief periods. Most colleges and universities have arrangements with a nearby hospital to accommodate students who need long-term hospitalization or surgery. The major activity of the student health centre is out-patient treatment, that is, the student who does not require hospitalization. In addition to a full-time medical staff most health centres have arrangements with specialists such as cardiologists, dermatologists, gynaecologists, neurologists and others to visit weekly and/or be available on call.

Institutions that have no campus housing and serve commuter students only usually have an abbreviated health service, perhaps only nurses who provide first-aid treatment and minor medical care. Students are expected to seek medical treatment away from the institution and most institutions arrange low-cost health insurance for their students. Increasingly institutions are limiting their care to limited service and requiring students to purchase health insurance to cover surgery and long-term hospitalization.

Career services and placement

This office assists both undergraduate and graduate students in obtaining employment as they near completion of their studies. Its services include testing and evaluation to determine occupations for which individuals are suited and not suited, providing information about hundreds of professions and occupations and occupational guidance and counselling. That office prepares résumés for students and posts these to prospective employers upon student request, arranges for employers to interview students, informs students as job vacancies occur and provides various other services.

Counselling services

Almost every college and university has a counselling centre, staffed by psychologists and trained counsellors to help students deal with their personal and emotional problems. Most academic advising is provided by a faculty member in the student's major field of study; some of it may be done by staff members in the office of the dean of the college in which the student is enrolled.

Counselling centre staff help students to deal with personal problems ranging from routine worries, boy friend and girl friend problems, adjustment to college, managing their time, relationships with others, sex problems and less serious and very serious emotional illness. Most counselling centres employ a psychiatrist, if not full-time, either part-time or on call.

Many young people away from home for the first time have adjustment problems that require professional help which these counsellors can provide. While most counselling centres concentrate on young students, as the average age of students rises, especially in urban colleges and universities, counsellors encounter more older students needing help with marital and family problems.

Student publications

On almost every campus in the US there is a student newspaper and student yearbook. The latter is a book size publication, often 9 by 12 inches, of 200 to 300 pages, containing photographs of students, by class, and photographs of students engaged in a variety of activities that are intended to depict student life. The student yearbook is published for nostalgia purposes so that years later students can re-examine and remember college days. In addition larger institutions have various other student-edited and produced publications, such as literary journals, humour magazines, publications that rate undergraduate courses and teachers, and more.

A key publication on every campus is the student newspaper. In some institutions only students studying journalism are allowed to serve on the editorial staff but on most campuses there is no such restriction. At some institutions the student newspaper is the voice of protest on campus, attracting to editorial positions students who wish to criticize society, the president of the institution and other administrators in the university and to practise investigative journalism. On others the student newspaper simply reports news; in between are many variations of papers.

Student newspapers are usually distributed free to students, faculty, administration and staff; costs of operation come from student service fees and advertising and are often subsidized by the institution. At a few institutions a charge is made for the paper.

Student editors on student newspapers with an investigative journalism bent often irritate the administration and board of trustees. Almost all student newspapers have a faculty adviser or an editorial board composed of students, faculty, administrators and sometimes professional journalists, but because of strong commitment in the US to freedom of the press, student editors are generally allowed broad freedom in deciding what to print. Administrators often contend that students do not have sufficient understanding of problems they write about or because of an anti-administration inclination, present only one side of a story. In addition student newspapers frequently rouse the ire of legislators, alumni and townspeople where the institution is located.

Organizations of university administrators have discussed from time to time possible courses of action to curtail irresponsible writing, but are reluctant to take any action that would subject them to a charge of infringement on freedom of the press. While student newspapers do not have the same legal status as commercial newspapers, they enjoy many of the same privileges.

At large institutions the student newspaper is published daily, Monday to Friday; in small institutions it is usually published weekly or twice a week.

Student government

A typical student government consists of a president, vice president and secretary-treasurer elected by students, plus a board or council consisting of representatives of colleges or, at a small college, departments. In some cases there is a student senate instead of a board, usually larger in number and consisting of representatives of colleges or departments, also elected by vote. When there is a board it is often composed of the student president or student officers of each college who sit by virtue of their election as college officers.

In a large university there are usually three officers for the college or frequently for each of the four classes of the college, for example, three officers — president, vice president and treasurer — for the senior class in engineering, three for the junior class, three for the sophomore class and three for the freshman class.

The primary function of student government officers and board members is to communicate to administrators and faculty suggestions and concerns of students, and that is essentially the function of college, department and class officers. The central student government, however, fills that role but also has many other responsibilities. At a large university the student body officers often receive salaries and because of the magnitude of their duties must reduce their course loads during the year of their service. As a minimum, student body government advises the administration concerning allocation of student service fees, and at many institutions the student government has complete authority to allocate all or a major portion of those funds. When we

168

consider the fact that student fees at an average size institution may total $2 million and at a very large university $5 million to $7 million annually, the magnitude of the student government's responsibility is apparent. It involves determining what portion is allocated for all student service activities, including campus clubs and societies, which may number fifty or more.

Student court

An important part of student government on many campuses is the student court, selected either by popular student vote or by the student senate to sit in judgment on many student violations of campus rules and regulations, such as theft, vandalism, cheating in examinations, plagiarism, violation of dormitory regulations and other misdemeanors. Decisions by the student court are always subject to review by the president of the university or his representative, but most presidents are inclined to concur with student court decisions unless the decision or action of the court is clearly inappropriate or contrary to state or federal law or institutional regulations.

Institutional governance

Student participation in governance grew rapidly during the 1960s and 1970s when students began to insist on being involved in decisions that go beyond those traditionally found within student government. Historically students have exercised considerable influence on matters relating to housing, food service, health service, clubs and organizations, intramural athletics, student discipline, recreation and entertainment through both official student government and on committees advisory to the vice president for student affairs or staff of that office.

In response to student insistence many colleges and universities added student members to the academic senate, to college faculty councils and to various committees. Students are usually appointed to university or college committees of faculty and administrators establish-ed to study institutional policies and procedures. They frequently sit on departmental committees concerned with hiring new faculty but rarely on committees concerned with faculty promotion or tenure. Many college deans and department chairmen have standing advisory committees of students.

Except in matters of student affairs, student influence on academic and other decisions is often more apparent than real. One reason is that students usually constitute a minority of committee membership. In addition they often know little about how the committee functions and lack experience and knowledge of how to get things done, in contrast to faculty members who may have served on the committee or on other committees for years. Students who accept committee appointments with alacrity sometimes find afterwards that they have too many time-conflicts or are not interested and therefore attend few meetings, often only those dealing with matters in which they are interested personally.

A large number of private and public colleges and universities now have student representatives on their boards of trustees. Twelve states have passed laws requiring that a student representative must serve on the board of trustees of each public college and university in the state and other institutions have student trustees without vote. While student trustees encounter the same conflict of interest problem as faculty, observers of student trustees report that for the most part they have performed their role responsibly.

Student subcultures

In small liberal arts colleges where most students know one another there is greater mixing of students from various backgrounds and with different interests. In larger institutions students tend to seek out others like themselves and to develop formal or informal associations. They aggregate on many bases — race, ethnicity, academics, wealth, social deviance, high school attended and a wide number of other interests.

Some of the typical subcultures are:

(a) students interested in athletics, either intercollegiate or intra-mural; sometimes called jocks, they devote most of their spare time to sports activities;

(b) Greeks or, more correctly, members of fraternities and sorori-ties who are sometimes accused of being frivolous and going to college primarily to have fun;

(c) politicians — these are usually involved in student government or manage the candidacy of students who seek student govern-ment offices; many of these later become state and national politicians;

(d) the intellectuals, sometimes unkindly referred to as grinds because they spend all their spare time studying with little or no recreation;

(e) anti-intellectuals — their objective is to pass their courses without studying and to use their time talking to other anti-intellectuals;

(f) the dissidents — these led the student revolution of the 1960s and while they are less active today and their numbers have declined sharply there is still a small coterie on many campuses, particularly in large urban universities.

On campuses where they are in the minority, blacks, Hispanics, Chinese-Americans and students from other countries assemble with others like themselves; they get reinforcement and are more comfortable with such associations, although these students, like other subcultures, mix with the entire student body in varying degrees.

During the 1960s and 1970s many students did not take their studies very seriously but the changing job market and competition for places in graduate school changed that. By the late 1970s only a few students did not take their studies seriously. They looked at the oversupply of people with degrees in the humanities, social sciences, fine arts, education and most other fields except business administration and engineering, and realized that only students with the best academic records would be admitted to the fewer places in graduate school, medical school and other professional schools and be offered the best jobs.

Graduate students generally take their studies even more seriously. A combination of education, maturity and career goals leads them to pursue their studies diligently, often adopting or assuming characteristics of faculty with whom they associate. The longer they continue in graduate study, working with professors in laboratories or as assistants, the more they come to share the faculty's opinions, values and lifestyle, commonly referred to as the process of socializing them into their profession or field of study.

Social activities

Social life and recreation play a major role in the lives of most undergraduates in American colleges and universities. Indeed some colleges have become famous (or infamous) as 'play schools' because their academic requirements are modest and opportunities for social life and recreation are attractive, but these are few in number and declining.

Fraternities and sororities

For many students social life centres around Greek letter social organizations — fraternities for men and sororities for women. These are quite distinct from Greek letter organizations that exist to honour academic, leadership or professional achievement, such as Phi Beta Kappa which honours academic achievement in the arts and sciences.

The first college social fraternity, Kappa Alpha, was founded in 1825 at Union College in Schenectady, New York. This was followed by the founding of other social fraternities and in 1850 Greek letter social organizations for women began to appear.

Each social fraternity and sorority is composed of members with common interests and similar backgrounds who share similar attitudes and values. The fraternity or sorority house, where members live and dine, is always located on or near the campus and is the centre of social activity.

Fraternities and sororities provide many social activities for their members — dances, dinners, parties and a variety of recreational and entertainment activities. They participate, as a group, in many kinds of campus competition such as intramural sports, debates, stunts, theatricals, and others. Each autumn at the annual homecoming celebration, usually on a Saturday when a football game is played, there is a parade on campus with floats (that is, exhibits mounted on cars, trucks, trailers and other vehicles) prepared by fraternities and sororities. Each fraternity and sorority usually holds open house after the parade for former members who have returned for the festivities. This provides an opportunity for undergraduates to meet members of their fraternity or sorority who have graduated and through such associations members often establish the beginnings of future social and business relationships and develop personal and professional friendships that endure.

Fraternities and sororities constitute support groups; members help one another with personal problems, tutor members who have academic difficulties, counsel one another concerning social behaviour, provide encouragement during periods of difficulty and help other members to develop a wider range of acquaintances among men and women on campus.

Before and after the evening meal members assemble in a social room for conversation and fellowship where friendships are developed and nurtured. Many friendships develop between members of a fraternity or sorority that last a lifetime. Members of the same fraternity or sorority often rely on those relationships later in life to help in business or professional practice or in politics. Members depend on fraternity 'brothers' or sorority 'sisters' to help establish social relationships with members of the opposite sex. Often a fraternity will join with a sorority to provide social activities for their members jointly on a continuing basis out of which grow close relationships between members of the two, including marriages.

The history of fraternities and sororities has been tumultuous. They grew rapidly in the late nineteenth century but at various periods in their history individual colleges and universities have closed or banned them. In earlier days some fraternities and sororities forbade membership of certain racial, ethnic or religious groups, which led to the founding of fraternities and sororities specifically for Catholics, Jews, blacks and other groups. In recent years virtually all fraternities and sororities that previously discriminated against these groups have eliminated such discrimination from their membership requirements. Some have made special efforts to recruit members of groups previously excluded but most have had limited success because individuals tend to choose to become members of social organizations with whose members they have mutual interests and whose values they share.

At the beginning of the autumn semester fraternities and sororities have a series of dinners and parties over a period of a week when potential members are entertained and current members get to know them to decide whether to invite them to membership. Most of the potential members are freshman students, each of whom will probably be entertained, known as 'rushing', by several fraternities or sororities.

A relatively small percentage of undergraduate students join social fraternities or sororities, between 10 and 15 per cent nationally. At some colleges and universities one-third to a half of undergraduates belong to fraternities and sororities but the figure is lower at most and some institutions have none. Most students who want to join a fraternity or sorority are able to do so although they may not be able to join their first choice. At some institutions the number of fraternities and sororities is inadequate for the demand and some students receive no invitation to membership; this occurs more often in the case of women than men students.

Most students choose not to join fraternities and sororities; some do not like the lifestyle, some are disinterested and some cannot afford to belong.

The debate over fraternities and sororities continues at many institutions and periodically a college will announce that it is banning them. On some campuses societies that serve similar purposes have developed in reaction against fraternities and sororities. At Yale University the senior societies developed with high selectivity for membership. At Princeton, eating clubs, also highly selective, were formed where members enjoy fellowship and establish friendships. At other colleges and universities various kinds of social clubs exist which, although they may have developed in reaction against them, serve many of the same purposes as fraternities and sororities. Most college and university administrators and faculty acknowledge the potential for fraternities and sororities to become excessively exclusive, élitist and to foster snobbery but feel that with proper guidance these can be minimized and that these societies are, on balance, a positive part of college life for many students.

Religious centres

On the campus or adjacent to it at most colleges and universities are found student religious centres, one for each denomination, a building that serves as a social centre for students of that religion and in which a limited amount of worship and religious education occurs. These are sponsored and financially supported by each religious denomination and each is often directed by a priest, rabbi or minister. The most thoroughly developed programmes are found in the centres sponsored by the Church of Jesus Christ of Latter Day Saints (Mormon) which provides extensive programmes of religious education for its members.

For many students these centres become the locus of most of their social life and provide the basis of social relationships. In short, it serves for them many of the purposes served by fraternities and sororities, although members of the latter also participate in programmes of the religious life centres.

Other social activities

The range of social, recreational and entertainment activities in American colleges and universities is as varied as the institutions themselves. Generally social activities are limited from Monday to Thursday evenings; Friday and especially Saturday evenings are usually devoted to parties, dances and other social events. In a small town most of these take place on the college campus, but when the institution is located in a large city, students go off campus for much of their recreation and entertainment. Even in cities, however, many social activities take place on campus.

With funds from student service fees, the student affairs office at each institution sponsors guest speakers on topics of current interest, movies of both current interest and of earlier years, local and touring musical groups and a wide variety of entertainment.

Sports

At American colleges and universities, sports, often referred to as athletics, are of two types and the distinction is important. Intramural sports involve competitive games among clubs, fraternities, sororities and other groups on a campus. Most popular are team sports such as softball, volleyball, basketball, touch football and soccer. Each year on most campuses, student organizations challenge one another for the campus championship in one or more sports and members of the players' organizations attend and cheer with gusto, but there is usually little attendance beyond the players' supporters. Admission to such games is free, there are no uniforms, coaches are student members of the organizations who receive no pay and such modest expenses as are incurred are borne by the organizations or by the university's student life office.

174

Intercollegiate sports

The fervour exhibited at a Saturday afternoon football game between Ohio State University and the University of Michigan, or any of dozens of other traditional rivals, is impossible to describe and difficult for anyone from another culture to comprehend. No leading state university is without a major football programme and presidents of those institutions would be reluctant to suggest de-emphasizing football for it would incur the wrath of many alumni and might well lead to a president's dismissal.

Most leading private universities also have strong football programmes but there are exceptions. The University of Chicago, once a football power, abolished it in the 1930s and appears to have weathered the step successfully. Harvard, Yale, Princeton, Cornell, Brown and several other leading private universities field creditable teams but make no attempt to win national championships. Many prestigious private institutions – a few universities and a large number of liberal arts colleges – play 'club sports' which include intercollegiate competition but on a much more modest scale with much less fanfare. Players receive no subsidy, coaches are often faculty who serve part-time as coaches without pay, playing achievements are modest, there is no radio or television coverage, attendance is usually small, and in general it is much the same as intramural competition.

A typical large university intercollegiate athletics programme includes not only football but also basketball, baseball, tennis, golf, track and field, swimming, boxing, wrestling and gymnastics. Soccer is growing in popularity, ice hockey is limited to a few institutions, principally in the northern part of the country, and lacrosse is found largely on the eastern seaboard. Women's teams have grown in recent years since the federal requirement that women be treated equally.

The traditional argument for intercollegiate athletics is that they build character, that the competition and related activity develop qualities in the players that will serve them well throughout life. While this is debatable, there are other undebatable reasons. Many young men who would otherwise have been unable to attend college have been able to do so by playing a sport. In most institutions with major athletics programmes players are provided with free tuition and fees, books, educational supplies, food and lodging, and modest stipends for incidental expenses. Earlier these were the sons of Polish, Irish, Italian and other immigrants; in recent years thousands of blacks have been able to attend college on scholarships for football and other sports. The National Collegiate Athletic Association has estimated that 110 000 students were receiving sports scholarships in the early 1980s worth $300 million annually, an average of more than $2700 per student.

In most states, government support of athletics is modest, not adequate to support strong teams; in others no tax income may be spent for intercollegiate athletics. The most powerful football universities realize sizable profits from football — admission fees, television broadcasts and incidental sales — enough to cover all the losses of minor sports, but most institutions are faced with the task of finding funds to pay for losses in athletic budgets.

The most compelling argument for athletics, particularly football and to a lesser extent basketball, is their public relations value — the goodwill and support the institution realizes from constituents. Many donors who might otherwise know little about the university become interested because of its success in football, and although some designate their gifts for athletics, more often they designate them for student scholarships, endowed professorships, buildings and other facilities. State legislatures sometimes seem to be more favourably disposed towards an institution if its football team has been successful.

Successful football teams appear in nationally televised games which bring the institution to the attention of potential students and faculty the institution would like to attract. In short, a successful football team can enhance an institution's success academically if managed properly.

Finally, successful sports teams build school spirit, enthusiasm, institutional loyalty and make students feel better about their institution and more satisfied with having chosen to attend that institution.

While violations of rules occasionally occur, voluntary (non-governmental) self-regulation keeps most of it under control. With the exception of a small number of independent institutions, most colleges and universities are members of regional conferences (associations) of eight to ten teams against whom they compete most often. All are members of one of two national associations — the National Collegiate Athletic Association or, in the case of institutions with smaller programmes, the National Association of Intercollegiate Athletics — which set rules of play and police teams' adherence to those rules.

The popularity of football is reflected in the attendance at games and the size of stadiums, mostly 40 000 to 75 000 seats with a maximum of 101 000 at the University of Michigan. Public interest is reflected in the fact that during the autumn football season, each Saturday afternoon and evening, national television networks and cable systems broadcast half a dozen or more college football games.

International students

American colleges and universities welcome students from other countries and they have come in substantial numbers for many years. In 1984—5 there were 338 890 students from other countries enrolled in American colleges and universities, of which 22 590 were from Taiwan, 21 720 from Malaysia, 18 370 from Nigeria, 16 640 from Iran, 16 430 from South Korea, 15 370 from Canada, 14 610 from India, 13 160 from Japan, 10 290 from Venezuela and lesser numbers from other countries, according to the Institute of International Education in New York City that assists students from other countries who come to America to study.

The leading institutions and the numbers of international students choosing those institutions in 1984—5 were: Miami-Dade Community College, Florida, 4316; University of Southern California, Los Angeles, 3716; University of Texas at Austin 3286; University of Wisconsin, Madison, 2901; Columbia University, New York City, 2773; Ohio State University 2606; North Texas State University 2570; Southern Illinois University, Carbondale, 2565; Boston University 2462; University of Houston (Texas), main campus, 2424. Virtually every college and university in the US enrols students from other countries. In 1984—5 seventy-six institutions enrolled 1000 or more foreign students each.

More than one-third were graduate students and just over one-third were enrolled in private institutions. One in eight was enrolled in a two-year college and almost one-third were women. About 23 per cent were studying engineering and 19 per cent were studying business administration. Approximately 42 per cent came from south and east Asia (*CHE*, 9 October 1985).

Almost all colleges and universities have a staff to assist international students. Known as the international student office or foreign student adviser, that office assists students from other countries with information before they leave home and then keeps in contact with them after they arrive, explaining how to obtain lodging, academic assistance and services and how to cope with a new and strange culture.

Once the privilege of the socially and financially élite, American colleges and universities are now open to virtually anyone who wants to attend. To be admitted to an academically prestigious institution requires high academic achievement and potential; however, less talented students may be confident of obtaining a good education in hundreds of less famous institutions.

Only a generation ago many young people were forced to forgo college because of lack of funds; today with the large array of federal and state grants, loan and work-study programmes and scholarships provided by institutions, corporations and individuals, lack of funds is no longer a barrier to college attendance.

Even though the percentage of the population with college degrees is growing and some of those degrees represent less than excellent education, a college education is still a major factor in upward social and economic mobility for the less privileged. While a college degree no longer carries the élitist image it once did, it is sought by a growing percentage of young people.

8 Research and public service

Providing courses and programmes leading to degrees is the main function of American colleges and universities but virtually all of them are involved in research and/or public service. Research is most prevalent in universities, to a lesser extent in liberal arts colleges and usually not at all in community colleges for which research is not a responsibility. Public service activities are most commonly found in public institutions but also in some private institutions, particularly in universities and comprehensive colleges, and to a lesser extent in private liberal arts colleges.

Public service encompasses a wide range of activities, including extension and continuing education. Many colleges and universities operate non-profit radio and television stations. In almost every state at least one public university provides consulting services and other forms of information and service to public schools. And many institutions have bureaux of economic research and service to assist business enterprises, governmental research and service to assist state and local governments, programmes to assist local communities in developing arts activities such as theatre and visual arts, and many more. In addition institutions provide specialized services to meet needs of their regions or states such as geological analyses, tourism promotion, water conservation, energy conservation and utilization, and others.

Community colleges usually serve only one city, town or community or a portion of a large city, and most of them receive at least part of their financial support from local taxes. These institutions are leaders in providing community services — non-credit courses to train skilled workers, community leaders, clerical and office employees and professional personnel, plus recreational and hobby courses; short-term conferences and workshops on almost any topic of interest to a group of people; assemblies of local citizens to discuss and debate local issues; studies of local problems; cultural and recreational activities, and others. Both public and private colleges and universities located in decaying cities have in many cases joined in efforts to solve urban problems and rebuild those cities.

According to the US Department of Education, in 1982–3 research and public service accounted for 11.8 per cent of all expenditures in American colleges and universities, not including the costs of operating hospitals associated with medical schools.

Research accounted for 8.7 per cent of expenditures in public institutions and 8.09 per cent in private institutions, with the largest portion in doctoral universities where research expenditures were 14.8 per cent in public institutions and 13.7 per cent in private institutions.

Public service accounted for 5.8 per cent of expenditures in public and 1.3 per cent in private doctoral universities; private liberal arts colleges spent only 0.8 per cent of their budgets on public service (*CHE*, 27 June 1984).

Research

Undergraduate education is concerned with the transmission of knowledge, and for students pursuing the master's degree transmission of knowledge is also the dominant function of universities. Most students pursuing the PhD degree are being trained to conduct research and part of that training involves participation in research conducted by their professors.

The conduct of research and publication of research findings is a responsibility of faculty in all universities and in most four-year colleges, as explained more extensively in Chapter 5. In some cases this responsibility is enunciated in the faculty member's contract but in most cases it is assumed; it appears most prominently in criteria for promotion, tenure and salary increase. Some institutions allot a limited amount of funds and a proportion of faculty time to research budgetarily but, typically, funds designated for a department for salaries and operating expenses are intended to cover both teaching and research. Except in community colleges and a few four-year colleges that do not expect them to conduct research, faculty's salary is assumed to cover not only teaching services but research and public service as well. In addition a portion of departmental operating funds is intended to cover research expenses, commonly referred to as departmental research as distinguished from research which is externally funded. Teaching loads are adjusted in keeping with the research expectations institutions make of faculty, as explained in Chapter 5.

Liberal arts colleges and comprehensive colleges and universities usually allot little, if any, funds for research; however, most doctoral universities are able to allot small sums, often to help a faculty member begin his research. A few affluent research universities, mostly private, are able to allot funds to pay a significant portion of research expenses. For the most part faculty must look to outside research grants and contracts, principally from the federal government, to finance research.

Organization for research

Most of the research in universities occurs as part of a faculty member's regular departmental assignment or through outside funding to the faculty member based on project proposals. However, many universities have established separate institutes, centres or other units for research. Among these are engineering experiment stations, centres or institutes of applied mathematics, child study, business and governmental research, social research, humanities research, and dozens of others. Some of the research institutes or centres are physically separated from teaching departments; in other cases they are fully integrated and the distinction between the teaching department and research institute is in record-keeping.

Separate research institutes and centres are often responsible to the academic department to which they are related but various arrangements exist. They may be responsible to the dean of a college, to the vice president for academic affairs or the dean of graduate studies. In universities with large amounts of externally funded research there is often an office responsible for monitoring all research in the university, especially the financial aspects, its role in the university and ensuring that all research complies with federal and state laws and ethical codes. Sometimes this office is headed by a vice president for research.

The faculty member who works in a research institute and is paid partly with funds budgeted to the institute is usually budgeted part-time in the academic department of his field of expertise where he teaches and directs graduate student research, although the research takes place physically in the research institute laboratory.

Research and graduate education

The training of researchers differs among different fields of study. In the humanities it is unusual for a faculty member to be able to obtain a research grant that will pay a graduate student a stipend and research expenses. As a consequence most doctoral dissertation research in the humanities is not funded; the student and professor meet periodically to review the student's research but for the most part the student works independently. This is also true of most dissertation research in the applied social science fields, except in applied psychology for which research grants and contracts are numerous, but to a lesser extent in business administration, social work, sociology and education.

In engineering and the natural sciences — basic and applied — more faculty members are able to secure research grants or contracts which include funds that are used to pay their doctoral students stipends to assist with the research. Typically the doctoral student assumes responsibility for solving a problem which is a part of the larger question being investigated by his professor and which becomes the student's dissertation. The student enjoys the benefits of funding — stipend, research expenses and close faculty guidance — but at the same time he has less autonomy in choosing the area of research and in conducting the study.

The student works daily in the laboratory on his research project and with his research supervisor, in a kind of apprenticeship role, learning to become a researcher. Through this relationship the student acquires not only the necessary research skills but is socialized into the discipline — attitudes, values, techniques and so on.

The percentage of PhD recipients who become full-time researchers outside universities is much higher in engineering and the natural sciences than in most other fields; students in those fields usually take less course work and devote more time to research in their graduate programmes than students in other fields.

The federal government and university research

All state governments provide funds to state universities and colleges for research, usually small amounts and often for research only in specified fields such as health and agriculture. The main source of funds for research in universities and colleges is the federal government, the large majority of it on a contract or grant basis rather than regular appropriations.

The federal government's involvement in research grew out of governmentally sponsored research during the Second World War. Before the First World War the government sponsored little research other than in agriculture. A modest beginning was made during the First World War and continued during the 1920s but funding sagged during the great depression of the 1930s.

In 1941 President Franklin D. Roosevelt created the Office of Scientific Research and Development (OSRD) which contracted with universities for research. OSRD developed policies and procedures for contracting with universities for research that set precedents for the major research efforts that were to follow the Second World War.

After the Second World War, OSRD was abolished but the foundation for federal support of university research had been laid. The National Institutes of Health had been established in 1930 but began to fund university research significantly after the Second World War. The Atomic Energy Commission was established and provided substantial sums for university research; it was later abolished and its functions assumed by other agencies, finally by the Department of Energy when it was established in 1977.

National science policy and federal support of research in universities began to solidify with the establishment in 1950 of the National Science Foundation (NSF), an independent federal agency, that is, not within a cabinet department, charged with responsibility for advancing scientific development. It is governed by an advisory board appointed by the President of the US, representing a wide spectrum of colleges and universities, industry and society at large.

The NSF modelled its approach to funding research on the Office of Naval Research — established in 1946 — which had developed a highly admired programme of research funding including studies not uniquely military such as personnel management, health, nutrition, and others.

All scientific research and development in the US involved expenditure of some $77 000 million in 1982 of which about half was spent by private industry and almost half by the federal government (Ad Hoc Committee, 1983). Approximately 10 per cent of all research and development was conducted in universities, but half the nation's basic research was done in universities. The federal government provides approximately two-thirds of the research and development funds received by universities, slightly more of the funds spent on basic research.

While industry accounts for half the research and development funds spent, much of that involves testing new products, either laboratory testing or field testing, for purposes of determining their commercial value and marketability.

Approximately 95 per cent of the federal funds allocated to colleges and universities for research come from six government agencies and departments: the Department of Health and Human Services, which includes the National Institutes of Health, the National Science Foundation, the Department of Defense, the Department of Energy, the National Aeronautics and Space Administration and the Department of Agriculture. About 70 per cent of the total is allocated through the National Science Foundation and the Department of Health and Human Services, principally the National Institutes of Health.

Most federally funded university research is in three categories:

1 Federally Funded Research and Development Centers (FFRDCs);
2 other research and development centres or institutes;
3 contracts and grants to individual faculty members in colleges and universities.

Of the thirty-two FFRDCs, nineteen are administered or managed by universities by contract with the federal government but are not integral units of the universities (six are administered by non-profit research institutes and the remainder by industry).

Some of the FFRDCs are administered by a consortium of universities, for example, the Brookhaven National Laboratory in New York State and the Oak Ridge Institute of Nuclear Studies in Tennessee. By definition an FFRDC is a separate unit or is separate from its sponsoring university or organization, performs research itself rather than subcontracting it, receives at least 70 per cent of its funds from the federal government and usually receives most of its funds from one government agency although it may perform research for several agencies. Five of the university-managed FFRDCs are astronomy observatories funded by the National Science Foundation, and twelve are multiple programme laboratories performing research for two or more federal agencies, but in each case they rely on one federal agency for most of their funds.

The FFRDCs have full-time research staffs, rather than using university teachers on a shared basis, and some are located a considerable distance from the sponsoring universities, for instance, the Los Alamos Scientific Laboratory in the state of New Mexico, which is administered by the University of California located 1500 km to the west. It conducts research for several federal agencies but primarily for the Department of Energy. The Jet Propulsion Laboratory, which conducts research for several federal agencies but primarily for the National Aeronautics and Space Administration, is located in Pasadena, California near California Institute of Technology, which administers it. On the other hand the Plasma Physics Laboratory at Princeton University and the Stanford Linear Accelerator are located at the universities that administer them.

While most of the research in the FFRDCs is conducted by resident staff scientists and engineers, faculty members and graduate students not only from universities that administer them but from other universities as well, are able to use the equipment and facilities for their own research. For some this means doing most of their research in the summer when they can be free from teaching obligations at their universities, if the FFRDC is located some distance away.

The second category of federal funding for universities, 'other research centres or institutes', also receive substantial sums of research funds from federal agencies. Some were formerly FFRDCs, for example, the Johns Hopkins Applied Physics Laboratory and the Applied Physics Laboratory at Pennsylvania State University which became integral units of their universities in 1978. Many other research centres and institutes on dozens of university campuses perform major research for federal agencies. They differ from FFRDCs in that they are integral components of their universities, their research staffs are likely to be professors who teach part-time while conducting research, and the centres and institutes may rely on either continuing contracts with federal agencies or on individually funded contracts and grants or both.

The third category of federal funding of university research consists of grants and contracts to individual faculty members by various government agencies, usually based on proposals submitted to the federal agency. Some federal departments and agencies rely principally on contracts in which the scientist performs research that is directed specifically towards solving problems the solutions to which are necessary for the missions of the funding agencies. Contracts usually involve much more monitoring than grants and involve considerable accounting by the university to the funding agency.

The National Science Foundation and the National Institutes of Health make most of their research awards in the form of grants. One of the foremost reasons is that much of the research these agencies fund is for basic studies in which the scientist needs freedom to pursue alternatives as they emerge. Basic research is not as amenable to control as applied research and development. The NSF awards approximately 12 000 grants each year; the NIH awards approximately 14 000 grants annually. Most grants to individual scientists at universities are for less than $150 000 a year and indeed many are for less than $50 000 (Ad Hoc Committee, 1983). Grants are usually for three year periods but with the tacit understanding that if the research is successful or shows promise funding is likely to be extended.

Government departments and agencies that fund research grants and contracts announce periodically the availability of funds for research, either in broad fields of inquiry or on specific topics related to a mission assigned to the agency by the Congress, and invite researchers to submit research proposals.

A typical project proposal includes a description of the research to be undertaken, how useful or important it is, how it applies to the objectives of the funding agency, a description of the research procedures, a list of facilities, equipment, personnel and other costs involved, the time required to complete the project, qualifications of the project director and other research staff and various other data. After all direct costs are determined, indirect costs are added to the proposed budget. These include general university costs of operation, applied proportionately to the research project, such as space, utilities, building cleaning and care, campus security, costs of servicing the project by the university's business office and other costs that affect the entire institution but are not budgeted to a single entity.

Indirect costs vary and are usually limited to a percentage of the total direct costs of the project or to salaries and wages of project staff, based on audits by federal accountants of similar research projects conducted previously in colleges and universities. According to the federal government's General Accounting Office, in 1982 indirect costs accounted for 30 per cent of all federal funds awarded to colleges and universities for research grants and contracts.

When research proposals are received by federal funding agencies, the staff assembles a panel of scientists or scholars who are leaders in the field, most of whom are university professors, to review the proposals and recommend those to be funded. The peer review process is intended to ensure that funding goes to those proposals that show most promise for success and for contributing to the agency's scientific objectives. As a consequence most federal research funds are awarded to universities that have assembled the most talented researchers. In 1982, 61 per cent of federal research funds allocated to higher education went to researchers in a hundred universities.

Faculty in less distinguished institutions argue that they are unable to gain prominence in research so long as the leading institutions receive most of the federal research funding. A few members of Congress have advocated allocation of federal research funds on a regional basis or ear-marking a portion of research funds for less competitive institutions. No formal action of this kind has been taken but staff members of funding agencies become concerned if institutions in a given region fare less well in competition for contracts and grants over a sustained period, particularly if that state or district is represented by a senator or representative who serves on the congressional committee that oversees the agency's funding.

Since junior faculty are at a disadvantage in national competition some federal agencies, for instance, the National Science Foundation, ear-mark a portion of their research funds for assistant professors. This serves the interests of the funding agency by developing a new crop of budding researchers from whom will come the research leaders of tomorrow.

In addition to current research expenses, the federal government provides limited amounts of funds for the purchase of equipment. During the 1960s and 1970s approximately half the cost of research equipment in universities was funded by the federal government, partly through direct grants to universities for the purchase of equipment and partly through research projects which called for special equipment not available at the university.

186

At various times the federal government has also provided subsidies for the construction of buildings and other physical facilities for research, as well as facilities for teaching and for libraries. Much of the support was in the form of interest subsidies on loans universities obtained from private lending agencies.

Beginning in the late 1950s the federal government began to provide fellowships for graduate students, particularly in the sciences and engineering but to a lesser extent in other fields as well. In the fiscal year 1981 the federal government allocated $215 million to fellowships, traineeships and training grants in science and engineering, with public and private universities each receiving approximately half the total. It should be noted, however, that by far the largest amount of federal support for graduate students in the sciences and engineering was in the form of research assistantships in which the student was paid a modest salary for part-time work, assisting a professor with a federally funded research project.

Private colleges and universities received approximately 42 per cent of funds allocated to higher education by the federal government for science and engineering in the early 1980s with public institutions receiving 58 per cent.

Federal agencies also support activities to disseminate research information to practitioners and other researchers. For example, sixteen Educational Resources Information Centers (ERIC) were established in the late 1960s and early 1970s to assemble research reports and other publications. Each specializes in a different area of education. About half the sixteen are located on university campuses and the remainder with other agencies; for example, the ERIC Clearinghouse on Rural and Small Schools at New Mexico State University, the Junior College ERIC at the University of California in Los Angeles, the Urban Education ERIC at Teachers College of Columbia University, the Tests, Measurement and Evaluation ERIC at the Educational Testing Service in New Jersey and the Teacher Education ERIC at the American Association of Colleges for Teacher Education in Washington, DC.

A National ERIC Center collects publications from each ERIC and from individual scholars, including both published and unpublished manuscripts, converts them into microfiche form and makes them available to university libraries and others at cost.

Several federal departments maintain research laboratories and installations staffed by scientists who are federal employees, especially the Department of Agriculture, the Department of Health and Human Services which operates several health research centres, the National Aeronautics and Space Administration, the Department of Defense and other agencies. However, the Department of Defense contracts with universities for most of its basic research but relies largely on industrial firms for applied research and development.

Agricultural research

The role of the federal government in university agricultural research merits special attention because of its place in the history of research. Before the passage of the Hatch Act in 1887 establishing an agricultural experiment station in the land-grant college of each state, the federal government sponsored no research. The success of the agricultural experiment stations in bringing about increased food production at lower costs was a major factor in the federal government's entrance into support of research in other fields of study.

The federal government operates several intramural agricultural and forestry research installations, notably the USDA Research Center at Beltsville, Maryland, fifteen miles from the nation's capital.

Most of the federal funds for research in agriculture appropriated by the Congress for the US Department of Agriculture are allocated to the agricultural experiment station associated with each state land-grant university. In 1981–2 the state agricultural experiment stations spent $995.257 million for research of which the federal government provided $387.557 million and state legislatures the remainder.

A major advantage of the programme of regular funding of state agricultural research by the federal government is that the scientists can depend on long-range support and plan their research accordingly. Consequently many studies are conducted involving breeding of new crop varieties, soil erosion control, reforestation, rebuilding dissipated organic matter in soils, and many others, that could not be done as well with short term contracts.

Since the state agricultural experiment stations are components of the colleges of agriculture in land-grant universities, the agricultural scientists usually divide their time between research and teaching, bringing to the classrooms the results of their research and involving graduate students in research.

Health research

Universities and colleges play a major role in research relating to health, and the federal government is the leading source of funds for such research. In the mid-1980s colleges and universities received approximately $5000 million from the federal government annually for research of which almost half was provided by the National Institutes of Health.

The National Institutes of Health, located in Bethesda, Maryland, in the suburbs of Washington, DC, were established by the federal government both to conduct research and to contract with universities and other institutions for the conduct of research. The National Institutes of Health include institutes concerned with: arthritis, musculoskeletal and skin diseases; ageing; allergy and infectious diseases; cancer; heart, lung and blood; diabetes, digestive and kidney diseases; dentistry; neurological disorders and stroke; the eye; child health and human development; environmental health; and general medicine. These twelve institutes conduct considerable research in their laboratories and hospitals in Maryland but most of the funds they receive are allocated to universities, non-profit hospitals and independent research institutes to conduct research on a contract or grant basis.

Medical schools and other health science programmes rely primarily on the National Institutes of Health for research funds, although state legislatures tend to provide more funds for health research than for any other category of research.

Non-governmental sources of funds

Non-profit foundations support research in all fields but are especially important to researchers in the social sciences and humanities, fields that receive only modest amounts of federal research support. In 1983 there were approximately 23 600 foundations in the US with assets totalling some $64 000.5 million which made grants of $4000.8 million.

Many of the larger foundations such as the Carnegie Corporation, the Rockefeller Foundation, Alfred P. Sloan Foundation, Ford Foundation, Danforth Foundation, Robert Johnson Wood Foundation and the Andrew W. Mellon Foundation are well known, have large endowments and are major supporters of research. There are many more that are less well known but which have several millions of dollars in assets and are important supporters of university research.

In addition a large number of corporations have established foundations to which the corporation's gifts are made and the foundations, in turn, allocate gifts or income from the endowment to philanthropic causes, including research. Among the leading ones are the General Motors Foundation, General Electric Foundation, Alcoa Foundation, Amoco Foundation, Monsanto Fund, TRW Foundation and Kresge Foundation.

Of the 23 600 foundations only 19 per cent had assets of $1 million or more in 1983. Most of the foundations with less than $1 million in assets were private, that is, foundations established by an individual or a family as a way of dispensing their philanthropy. Often the governing boards and the officers of such foundations are family members. Such foundations are created in order that an individual or family may establish an endowment whose income can be used for ever to support activities of interest to the individual or family. Tax laws encourage foundations to give almost all the annual income of the endowment as it is received rather than allowing it to accumulate which means that virtually all these foundations are continuously active in making grants. With other small foundations, the family foundations support many activities, including research, that might otherwise go unfunded, especially research on problems of handicapped children, mental illness, social welfare, educational innovation, gerontology, crime, regional economics and many other problems. Some faculty members whose research interests coincide with those of small foundations establish relationships with the governing boards or officers that lead to research support over a period of many years.

Business and industry also support a considerable number of university research projects, a few on a continuing basis but in most cases on a special project basis. Some industries rely primarily on universities to conduct research needed; in some cases it is less costly, in others the industries need to be able to assure customers that the research was unbiased and in some cases the research calls for expertise which the firm cannot employ.

Projects supported by business and industry tend to be of shorter duration than those supported by governmental agencies and deal with problems of immediate concern to the firm. Business and industry provide less than 5 per cent of university research funds but such funds tend to be largely in business administration and engineering where they constitute important sources of research support. However, pharmaceutical manufacturers provide a considerable share of funds for research by professors in schools of pharmacy. Geologists rely on oil companies for some research support, economists receive research support from investment and financial firms, and chemists receive a minor, yet significant, amount of research support from the chemical manufacturing industry.

Research outside the university

Far more manpower and money are spent on research outside universities than within them. Every major business and industrial enterprise in the country conducts research, ranging from the small bank that has one employee who assembles statistics on which the bank officers can base decisions to the Dupont Corporation which employs thousands of scientists, including hundreds of chemists with PhD degrees, to conduct research on chemicals and other products. International Business Machines and other electronics firms spend millions of dollars annually on research. Most business leaders agree that a company that fails to invest in research will eventually fall behind its competitors and is likely to go out of business.

While business and industry contract with universities for a portion of their research, most of it is done by their own research staffs for several reasons. A major one is secrecy, the need to maintain privacy until the product or process is developed and refined and can be patented, providing the company with exclusive use or control of the discovery for seventeen years.

A major component of the American research effort is the non-profit independent research institute or foundation, of which there were 400 in 1985. Most have been established in or near major cities or universities and conduct research for federal and state governments, for business and industry, and others on a contract basis. Some depend solely on income from research contracts for financial support, others are endowed and some depend in part on dues from industry members or contributors.

Some independent research institutes specialize in economic and management studies; others concentrate on engineering, metals and other materials; some specialize in testing new products; some do research on policy matters for the federal government; and others accept contracts for research on a wide range of topics.

Among some of the better known ones are the Battelle Memorial Institute in Ohio, the Rand Corporation in California, the Midwest Research Institute in Missouri, the Brookings Institution in Washington, DC and the Southwest Foundation for Research and Education in Texas.

Several independent non-profit research institutes began as Federally Funded Research and Development Centers and other university research and development units funded by the federal government, including some of the better known ones. Columbia University's Electronics Research Laboratory became the Riverside Research Institute; Stanford Research Institute left Stanford University to become SRI International; and the Instrumentation Laboratory at Massachusetts Institute of Technology changed its name to Charles Stark Draper Laboratory in 1973 and became independent of MIT.

Private industry turns to these independent non-profit research organizations for much of its research because they can treat research findings in confidence, in contrast to many universities that will not accept a research contract that places limitations on publication of findings.

Universities have been instrumental in helping to establish research parks near their campuses. One of the leading ones is located near Stanford University; another is the Research Triangle in North Carolina located in a wooded area within a triangle consisting of Duke University, the University of North Carolina at Chapel Hill and North Carolina State University. Both private industry research units and non-profit research institutes locate in the research parks, concentrating into a single location a wealth of intellectual talent. Universities benefit in several ways from having such research parks nearby: scientists with the research laboratories provide valuable assistance to universities through lecturing part-time and directing graduate student research, the laboratories provide part-time employment for students and full-time jobs when they complete their studies and employees often become part-time students.

The first cooperative industrial research undertaking occurred in 1983 when twelve computer manufacturers — later more than twenty — joined to form the Microelectronics and Computer Technology Corporation (MCC) to conduct basic research in computing, with a view to pursuing jointly research that no single company could afford. Industries had previously refrained from such cooperation in the belief that it violated federal restraint of trade laws but MCC was able to structure itself to avoid that problem.

Research in the private sector also includes thousands of profit-making enterprises, including market research firms, economic analysts, opinion polling organizations and many that conduct the same kinds of research as that done by independent non-profit research institutes and laboratories.

Extension and continuing education

Federal legislation in 1914 established the Agricultural Extension Service as a part of the land-grant college in each state, charged with the responsibility of bringing to farm families the results of agricultural research. It also included homemaking and later added programmes for youth (4-H Clubs — head, heart, hands, health) that supplement formal education in schools.

The Agricultural Extension Service, known in some states as the Cooperative Extension Service (meaning cooperation between the federal and the state governments), employs college graduates in agriculture and home economics who are stationed in each county of every state to provide information to farmers and other rural residents through a variety of approaches including public lectures, demonstrations and other meetings, newsletters, radio and television, and to individuals who visit the Extension offices or visits by Extension agents to farms and homes and by telephone. As the number of American farms declined Agricultural Extension agents expanded their services to urban residents with emphasis on lawns, trees, flowers and shrubs; insect and pest control; wildlife development and control; maintenance and repair of homes and other buildings and other topics.

Graduates in home economics stationed in each county originally limited their services to farm women, providing information on food processing and preparation, home management, textiles and clothing and related matters, but they too have expanded their services to instruction for residents of towns and cities and to include child care and rearing, nutrition, health and other matters not peculiar to rural residents.

Youth agents (4-H Club) on the county Extension staff provide informal instruction to teenage and pre-teen youth not only in farming and homemaking but in citizenship and personal development. Originally the agents worked with farm youth only but in recent years have expanded their services to non-farm youth as well and deal with many non-farm and non-homemaking topics; however, farm youth continue to be the primary clientele for 4-H club programmes.

County Extension staffs are supported by a staff of specialists in the Agricultural Extension Service headquarters of the college of agriculture at the state's land-grant university who interpret research findings and translate them into forms that farmers and others can use. They are the link between researchers and the county Extension agents.

Each year, in its appropriations for the US Department of Agriculture, the Congress provides funds for allocation to each state's Agricultural Extension Service, an amount for each state which must be matched by state-appropriated funds. State and county governments provide, on average, about two-thirds of the Agricultural Extension Service budgets; in 1983—4 the state Agricultural Extension Services spent $947.053 million of which $612.712 million was provided by state and county governments and the remainder by the federal government.

Other extension programmes

Many universities, particularly state universities, offer a variety of extension and continuing education activities for non-farm clientele. Some extension programmes grow out of interests of individual professors or academic units within universities, but the leading public universities in each state, and often other public universities as well, usually have colleges or schools of extension and continuing education, sometimes called divisions of general extension, headed by deans, who are responsible for coordinating all extension activities of the institution except agriculture and home economics. They conduct conferences on the university campus and sometimes at off-campus locations on topics such as banking, industrial management, real estate, accounting, management, legal matters, health care, social work, problems of local government and many more.

Extension and continuing education usually denotes non-credit instruction, that is, teaching not applicable to a college degree, usually consisting of one, two or three days of instruction on a given topic, no examinations, and oriented towards problems that may not be appropriate for college level courses. On the other hand the division of general extension in many institutions also conducts formal courses, usually in the evenings and on Saturdays, that are applicable to college degrees. Some provide college credit courses through correspondence and a few conduct instruction on television that may be applied to requirements for a degree.

Unlike the Agricultural Extension Service which is supported financially by the federal and state governments, general extension programmes are usually self-supporting, at least in part. State governments often pay the cost of maintaining an administrative staff for a college or division of general extension, but most, and frequently all, the cost of instruction is obtained from enrolment fees.

Colleges of engineering in several land-grant universities provide extension services but on a much more limited basis than the Agricultural Extension Service. None has staff stationed in each county in the state; instead they dispatch engineering specialists to lecture throughout the state and, more often, arrange special conferences at the university.

Some states require professional practitioners to pursue continuing education periodically to maintain their licences. Some examples: physicians 29 states; veterinarians 26 states; certified public accountants 46 states; pharmacists 36 states; dentists 13 states; attorneys 20 states (*CHE*, 21 May 1986).

University press

As in other countries American universities have established book publishing divisions to publish scholarly and scientific books that commercial book publishers do not consider financially profitable undertakings. Occasionally a book published by a university press will become a best-seller but this is rare and most books from university presses do not sell enough copies to make a profit.

In many cases the university press must be subsidized by the university of which it is a part in order to remain in business. The cost of publishing books has driven many university presses out of business and others have survived only by joining with other university presses in joint or cooperative enterprises, for example, the University Presses of Florida.

There are approximately a hundred university presses in the US, including the joint or cooperative presses. Among the leading university presses of private universities are those at Chicago, Harvard, Princeton, Yale and Stanford, and among the leading ones in state universities are

California, Texas, North Carolina, Illinois, Oklahoma, Nebraska and Louisiana State.

Both the Oxford University Press and Cambridge University Press are prominent in the US, not only in terms of sales but in publishing books written by Americans.

In assessing the status and prestige of an American university the presence of a thriving university press is a decided asset, influenced by the quality of books and journals the press publishes. One of the more prolific university presses in the US adds little to the prestige of the university because it concentrates on one field and the books are aimed more at the trade market than the scholarly community. On the other hand Johns Hopkins University and the University of Chicago both established high academic reputations immediately after their founding in the latter part of the nineteenth century, partly because of the establishment of university presses that published a number of highly regarded scholarly journals. The University of Chicago Press continues to publish the largest number of books annually and the largest number of scholarly journals of any American university presses.

Other public service

There are approximately 1200 non-profit radio stations in the US of which about 60 per cent are located on college and university campuses. Many are low-powered stations that reach only campus residents but most have enough power to reach the entire city and often a hundred miles or more. These stations are usually operated by students, more often students pursuing degrees in radio-television or journalism, and since they are non-profit enterprises their programming is not designed to secure large audiences. Most of the stations try to provide cultural, educational and entertainment programmes not available on commercial stations. Some such stations have a policy of not broadcasting music that is available on commercial stations and in many towns and cities the university or college radio station is the only station providing classical music daily.

In addition to local programming, campus radio stations may broadcast programmes prepared by National Public Radio in Washington, DC, a non-governmental organization supported financially by member stations and grants from the Corporation for Public Broadcasting.

Of the approximately 300 public non-profit television stations in the US about a quarter are affiliated with colleges and universities. Due to high costs most colleges and universities cannot afford the capital outlay required for a television station nor the annual operating expenses. Although campus television stations are used for teaching courses as well as informal education and information, their programming format in the evening is similar to that of other non-profit television stations, all of which depend on the Public Broadcasting Service (PBS) for part of the programmes they broadcast. PBS is a non-governmental association created to provide programming service to its member stations.

The Public Broadcasting Service receives most of its financial support from the Corporation for Public Broadcasting, an independent agency of the federal government established by the Congress specifically to allocate funds to PBS and to monitor the spending of those funds. This arrangement relieves the Congress of having to monitor public television and of direct interference in its activities and programming. A board of citizens manages the Corporation for Public Broadcasting and negotiates with the Public Broadcasting Service. Federal appropriations to the Corporation for Public Broadcasting are constantly the subject of controversy not only among some members of the Congress but citizens as well, who believe that PBS public affairs programmes are predominantly of one political ideology.

Local public television stations receive most of their funds from voluntary contributions by viewers. At least twice a year each station dedicates several days to fund raising through a variety of strategies but primarily through appeals to viewers to become members, that is, make contributions. Such contributions may be deducted from the donor's income when computing federal and state income taxes. In a few states, state governments provide subsidies to all public television stations within those states, and in several states all stations share programming costs through a cooperative public broadcasting network within the state.

Research and public service have been part of American higher education for more than a century, epitomized in the land-grant college movement and since then spreading to all public and most private institutions. Some educators feel American colleges and universities have taken public service too far, that it occupies an inordinate amount of faculty and administrator time and university resources, and that it has come to involve some activities inappropriate for higher education.

The accomplishments of university researchers during the Second World War and afterwards, the success of land-grant colleges of agriculture in improving the production of food and fibre, and other notable achievements in research and public service led the public to believe universities could solve almost any problem. During the 1960s and 1970s federal, state and local governments turned to universities to solve their most difficult problems — those involving deteriorating inner cities, race relations, pollution and environmental abuse, foreign policy, poverty, and many more. But these were problems that universities could not solve, at least not to everyone's satisfaction nor as quickly as an impatient governmental agency desired, and many people became disenchanted with higher education. Many government leaders and citizens generally had imputed to universities the ability to solve problems that are beyond the competence of higher education and probably beyond the competence of any agency or organization. At the same time universities had oversold themselves, leading the public to believe them to be capable of all things. In the late 1970s public confidence in higher education waned but by the mid-1980s it appeared to have been largely restored, if not to some of its earlier levels, to more realistic perceptions of what colleges and universities can do.

None the less the American public has become accustomed to its colleges and universities being actively involved in service activities and the institutions are not likely to abandon that role nor to reduce their service activities significantly. Public institutions, in particular, are considerably responsive to legislative and other political influences and would be unable to diminish their service role if they wished, and there is little evidence that they wish to do so. In addition to a philosophical commitment to the service role, most college and university faculty, administrators and trustees recognize the importance of both research and public service in maintaining public support for their institutions.

References

A Guide to Education for the Health Professions, Acropolis Books, Washington, DC, 1979.

Ad Hoc Committee, *Strengthening the Government-University Partnership in Science*, National Academy Press, Washington, DC, 1983.

Anderson, Charles J., *1981–82 Fact Book for Academic Administrators*, American Council on Education, Washington, DC, 1981.

Astin, Alexander, *et al.*, *The American Freshman: national norms for fall 1982*, Cooperative Institutional Research Program, University of California, Los Angeles, 1982.

Astin, Alexander, and Lee, Calvin B.T., *The Invisible Colleges*, McGraw-Hill, New York, 1972.

Brubacher, John S., and Rudy, Willis, *Higher Education in Transition: a history of American colleges and universities, 1636–1965*, Harper and Row, New York, 1958.

Centra, John A., *Faculty Development Practices in US Colleges and Universities*, Educational Testing Service, Princeton, NJ, 1976.

Chronicle of Higher Education, 1 September 1977; 16 January 1978; 12 October 1983; 22 February 1984; 4 April 1984; 30 May 1984; 27 June 1984; 25 July 1984; 12 September 1984; 3 April 1985; 17 April 1985; 8 May 1985; 17 July 1985; 4 September 1985; 9 October 1985; 18 December 1985; 15 January 1986; 12 February 1986; 19 March 1986; 23 April 1986; 7 May 1986; 21 May 1986; 16 August 1986.

Curti, Merle, and Nash, Roderick, *Philanthropy in the Shaping of American Higher Education*, Rutgers University Press, Rutgers, NJ, 1965.

Eels, Walter Crosby, and Haswell, Harold A., *Academic Degrees: earned and honorary degrees conferred by Institutions of Higher Education in the United States*, Bulletin 1960, no. 28, OE-54008A, US Office of Education, republished by Gale Research Co., Detroit, Mich., 1970.

Flexner, Abraham, *Medical Education in the United States and Canada*, Carnegie Foundation for the Advancement of Teaching, New York, 1910.

Gouldner, Alvin, 'Cosmopolitans and locals: toward an analysis of latent social roles', *Administrative Science Quarterly*, December 1957, pp. 281—303; March 1958, pp. 445—67.

Kerr, Clark, *Uses of the University*, Harvard University, Cambridge, Mass., 1963.

Ladd, Everett Carll, and Lipset, Seymour Martin, *The Divided Academy: professors and politics*, McGraw-Hill, New York, 1975.

Levine, Arthur, *Handbook on Undergraduate Curriculum*, Jossey-Bass, San Francisco, 1978.

Montgomery, David C., 'The encouragement of summer enrollment', *College and University*, 57:4 (Spring 1982), pp. 353—64.

Three Thousand Futures, Final Report of the Carnegie Council on Policy Studies in Higher Education, Jossey-Bass, San Francisco, 1980.

Voluntary Support to Education, Council on Financial Aid to Education, New York City, 1979—80.

In the interest of brevity and readability and since this book is aimed primarily at the general audience of which many readers would not be interested in further investigation of sources, citations have been limited.

Index